The Architect's Guide to Running a Job

for M & M

The difficulty about a gentlemen's agreement is that it depends on the continued existence of the gentlemen.

The Architect's Guide to Running a Job

Fifth edition

RONALD GREEN, FRIBA AADip FCSD

With a foreword by Sir Hugh Casson

Architectural Press

Butterworth-Heinemann
Linacre House, Jordan Hill, Oxford OX2 8DP
225 Wildwood Avenue, Woburn, MA 01801-2041
A division of Reed Educational and Professional Publishing Ltd

A member of the Reed Elsevier plc group

OXFORD   AUCKLAND   BOSTON
JOHANNESBURG   MELBOURNE   NEW DELHI

First published by The Architectural Press Ltd 1962
Fourth edition 1986
Fifth edition 1995
Reprinted 1996, 1997, 1998

British Library Cataloguing in Publication Data
Green, Ronald
    Architect's Guide to Running a Job. -
    5Rev.ed - (Butterworth Architecture
    Management Guides)
    I. Title   II. Series
    692.80941

ISBN 0 7506 2206 7

Printed and bound in Great Britain by MPG Books Ltd, Bodmin, Cornwall

Contents *in practice sequence*

Foreword

By Sir Hugh Casson

First—in fairness to the reader—I must declare an interest. The author of this book has been for many years a colleague and partner, and all of us with whom he has worked have personally learned much from his experience and skill in administration, the principles of which he has now been persuaded to set down in print for the benefit of the profession in general.

Much has been said and written in the past few years—and not before it was time—about the profession's apparent reluctance or inability to face up to its administrative responsibilities. The belief has been allowed to grow up that good art and good administration are incompatible. A good designer to many people means an architect who cannot be trusted to keep to a budget or a programme. An able administrator implies ignorance of or indifference to visual matters. Neither charge is wholly untrue. Neither does the profession credit. Both undermine the architect's claim to be the leader of the building team. The truth—the truism if you like—is that (as the author remarks) designing and administration are integral parts of a job—each of which demand, and must receive, a proportion of everybody's time in the office, whether he be the senior partner or the most junior draughtsman. The architect has a duty to the client to run a job efficiently. Equally important is his duty to himself to spend no more time upon it than is needed to ensure that it is done properly and well. This is exactly what this book is designed to help us achieve. Here you will find, set out in correct sequence—from the brisk ice-cold commonsense of its opening paragraph to the final warm-hearted words of parting advice—and without recourse to management jargon, all the many operations from site inspection to briefing a mural painter, from party-wall procedure to the nomination of sub-contractors, that may be met with in running a job of any size from any office, large or small. As a reference book, information chart or check-list, it will be found invaluable.

Note to fifth edition

The objectives of this book are clear from the introduction though since its first publication alternative ways of commissioning buildings have been adopted which make the identification of the historically conventional route from design to completion, under the direction of the architect, only one of many being practised today.

As in earlier revisions of this book this has led to a reduction in reference to specific documentation. It is assumed that the reader will look to other books or publications for detailed information related to alternative routes or procedures.

With this route, however, the underlying pattern remains the same for commissions which require the architect to steer the work through from enquiry to occupation. The present training of an architect and the required level of qualification to permit the use of the title assumes this to be the case.

Ways and means will change but the constants will all require attention if the translation of the design from two into three dimensions is to provide a building which both satisfies the client's needs and produces a piece of architecture.

Introduction

A client commissions an architect to produce a well-balanced building in terms of appearance, planning, construction, initial and maintenance costs. He expects an efficiently run contract and an amicable settlement of final account. In many cases, the client is an extremely efficient business organization and expects the contract to be run in a similar manner. In order to achieve this, an architect is faced not only with organizing his own office, but also relying on the support of scores of competitive sub-contractors, half a dozen main contractors, the quantity surveyor, the engineer and any specialists who are involved. Up to now this has generally resulted in his becoming one of two things: a designer who hopes that it will be accepted that he is not very good at administration, or an administrator who, as a result, does little designing. At best he pushes on hoping that the details will sort themselves out on the site.

Designing and administration are each an integral part of the job and demand a proportion of time to be spent on them which, with some exceptions, should not vary enormously from job to job. The method by which a design is developed and brought into shape as a building is through the application of a set of administrative constants which are the known quantities of nearly all contracts. The most common form of trouble is the failure to apply these administrative 'musts' in a sequence which anticipates the steps which follow. This reacts throughout the whole contract, resulting in a cumulative muddle which can only be remedied at the expense of design time.

If these events can be put down in their true order, referred to at the appropriate time, dealt with and forgotten, the most economical pattern of contract administration falls into place. On this basis, each of the following pages represents one phase in the sequence of operations, and line diagrams summarize the text for the sake of easy reference. Occasionally, on some of the pages, a certain amount of repetition has become necessary in order to make the context more clear.

A system for administering contracts must not inflict an unwieldy form-filling discipline on an office, taking more time than it saves on a contract. It can only be a framework within which a practice can operate according to its own personality. A thoroughly well-organized architect will probably fill out the framework with supplementary information—others may only regard it as a way of eliminating the interminable internal memos beginning 'Don't forget . . .'

1

Preliminary enquiries

Do not assume that because you are approached by a client it necessarily means that you will be commissioned to carry out the work or, indeed, that you want it. Because architecture is such a personal thing the immediate reaction is to be flattered that anyone has come at all, but one cannot afford to be led astray by this. If you have never met him before, it may be blatantly obvious at the first meeting that you are not his man, or alternatively that he is not yours. If the client has come on recommendation, he may not have seen your work, and even if he has seen it he may not appreciate the nature of the work or the costs involved, including fees for yourself and for consultants. The corporate client will often be well versed in briefing an architect; but do not discount the possible need to explain the architect's job in detail to the individual client so that he sees the importance of his own role.

It is essential to discuss terms of appointment, programme of work and costs with your client at the outset so that you both understand all the implications. The results will depend largely upon this. Your client must be given the opportunity to consider your approach to the problem and his commitment after these meetings.

Similarly, if you do not feel entirely sympathetic with his views at this stage, you must make it perfectly clear and offer to recommend another architect.

This is the time to be absolutely honest with yourself and your client and consider the following points carefully:

Competence: Can you deal with the type of work required by your client, or should you recommend people who are better used to it?

Commitments: Can you carry it financially? Will your other commitments permit you to devote adequate staff and time to the work? There is no point in telling a client that you can do a job, knowing that you cannot start it for three months. You must tell him this. He may be prepared to wait.

Complications: The RIBA recommended conditions of appointment are a sound and accepted basis on which to conduct an architectural commission. Look with caution at any suggested modification of these arrangements.

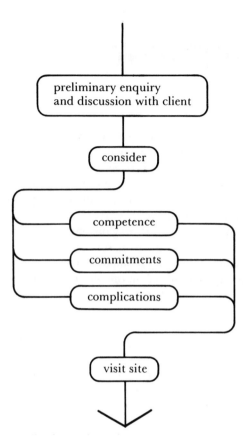

2
Office programme

Unless staff are to be taken on specifically to deal with a job, programming for it should take account of other work running concurrently and of the demands on all staff, including principals and secretaries.

While planning for the inevitable contingencies (illness, holidays, local authority hitches), remember that delays are cheaper for the client before the quantities are prepared rather than after work has commenced on the site. Now is also the time to check the job's likely contract value against the office current professional indemnity cover.

The programme should be drawn up in the following phases and, before issue, checked by your client and by everyone in the office who will be concerned with the job:

phase 1 Survey
2 Briefing and analysis
3 Design
4 Consents
5 Production/contract drawings
6 Quantities
7 Tenders
8 Construction
9 Defects liability
10 Final settlement

It is at this stage that you should consider which, if any, of the following consultants should be employed, and their part in the programme.

Surveyor: When accurate site information is not to hand or when converting an existing building where no survey exists.

Quantity Surveyor: If the cost of the works is likely to exceed the ceiling beyond which contractors are unlikely to tender in competition without bills of quantities. These documents, while acting as the basis of accurate cost comparison for competitive tenders and post-contract costing, form one part only of a cost control operation provided by a quantity surveyor from design briefing to completion. It is for the wider service that you would suggest such an appointment.

Consultant Engineer: For work of structural complexity.

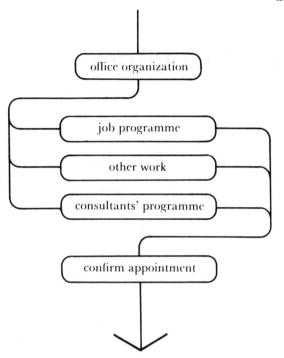

Mechanical and Electrical Services Consultant: Where complex environmental control, communications systems or other similar services are involved.

'Specialists' of any kind: Where decorative, interior, sculptural, graphic or other similar works are proposed.

This is also the stage at which the client must be made aware of his obligations under the Construction (Design and Management) Regulations to appoint a planning supervisor whose duties will be related to health and safety aspects of the work.

3
Conditions of engagement

The services required of an architect between being invited to undertake a building design from briefing to completion of the final account have over many years been proved to correspond with those which are outlined in the RIBA document describing the services of an architect. The process as defined there has shown itself to be the sensible minimum within which the architect can achieve the client's objectives. Time and experience have also shown that fees charged as a percentage of the contract value of the building have borne a consistent relationship with the scope of this service, though naturally these will prove themselves to be inadequate, adequate or profitable depending upon the degree of efficiency which the architect is able to apply to the commission.

It is of no benefit to a client if you offer him a reduced cost to secure work which will then require the full service required of a normal commission. In the case of a client wishing to reduce professional costs at the outset, it is in the best interests of both the architect and the client to agree an appropriate level of reduction in the normal service. Partial services may be perfectly satisfactory for the particular type of commission the client has in mind, and so long as the level of work required is related to an intelligently assessed sum within which it can be provided, there is no reason why the architectural service cost should not be negotiated with the client.

Partial services are frequently provided on the basis of time charges at an hourly rate agreed in advance. Staff costs can be assessed from the salary and overhead costs to an office, but the principal rate is generally based on a calculation which assumes that of 220 actual seven-hour working days in a year totalling 1,540 hours, about 1,100 of these can be actively used on a client's business where the professional is also involved as a principal, conducting the additional everyday duties of running a practice. The cost of the principal's time per hour is therefore broadly based upon this method.

The inexperienced or newly qualified architect assessing charges early in his practice career would do well to consider the situation very carefully before departing from the traditional terms of appointment. The law requires a particular level of competence from a person practising as a qualified architect (the title Architect identifying in the United Kingdom a person registered under the Architects Registration Act) and a client is entitled to expect it. This level can be maintained only by charging a fee which ensures that the practitioner can remain in practice to provide the service which fulfils the obligation.

It is not unusual for a client to look to the architect to provide an 'all-in service' in order to secure a single source of both contact and cost for professional services. Unless the practice provides these multi-disciplinary services this means that the client is looking to the architect to employ the engineer, the quantity surveyor and the services consultant directly. If the architect does so he must accept direct responsibility to his client for the work under the consultant's direction, so in turn he would require indemnity from each of the consultants for the work they do within the global arrangement.

4

Architect's appointment

It is said that a contract can exist by word of mouth when it is evident that the two parties recognize an agreement to exist between them, but the dangers from misunderstanding are enormous, so following the preliminary discussion, a letter of confirmation should be sent to your client setting out the agreed terms of appointment. It should be borne in mind that this letter and/or a letter from your client, in the absence of a formal agreement, may be the only document which could be referred to as a contract. Being a potential legal document, it must anticipate all the snags which could arise from loosely-drawn terms of appointment.

The letter should:
1 Check that no other architect has been instructed or is working on the same project.
2 State clearly the brief as you understand it if the work is fairly simple or the objectives which future briefing meetings will aim to satisfy.
3 Inform your client of other professional services or consultants required and of how they are appointed and paid.
4 Recommend such specialists for interior, sculptural, graphic or other similar work as you consider necessary.
5 Check if there is a survey available and, if not, arrange with your client the immediate appointment of a surveyor.
6 Advise your client that he will need a clerk of works if he wants full time inspection of the work on the site.
7 Advise your client of his obligations to comply with all statutory regulations, where necessary obtain consents, and also appoint a planning supervisor to deal with the health and safety aspects in accordance with the Construction (Design and Management) Regulations.
8 Check that he agrees with the draft programme for the work.
9 Advise him of any negotiations which may be necessary with the adjoining owners and of the financial implications.
10 Enclose conditions of appointment and describe the scope of your services, fees, expenses and time of payment so that he can assess commitments at the start.
11 Ask the client to appoint a staff representative with authority to take day-to-day decisions if your client is a committee.

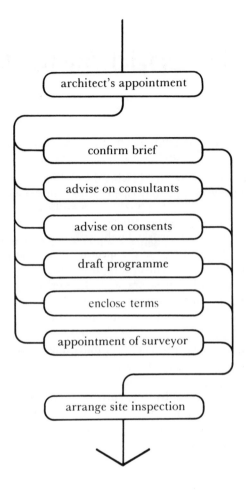

Your client should be made aware of all these points at this stage so that he can plan his own programme in terms of leasehold or other arrangements on present properties, and anything else likely to affect occupation of a new building.

5
Client's project management

Under the terms of the average commission and in the customary use of the majority of building contracts, the architect is required to undertake a leading role and to co-ordinate the work of other professionals in the team. The conventional terms of appointment assume a direct relationship with, and responsibility towards the client which permits the architect to conduct a commission with this appropriate level of authority. The result depends upon it.

A client equally has a duty to work closely with the architect in defining as clearly as possible the requirements of the project. With a corporate client this is generally done by the secondment of a representative, who speaks with the authority of the client's board of directors, and who works with the architect and professional team from day to day, clarifying all the issues under discussion. For a large project this requires the full time attention of a member of the client's staff. In the first instance his is an interpretative and advisory role. Through this person the architect gains access to responsible individuals in the company whose opinions are important to the progress of the project, whether as members of the Board, senior staff with departmental responsibility, or members of staff whose work has specific requirements. In time this representation becomes a wider management function and develops into a liaison role between consultants and the client in identifying and resolving matters concerned with the monitoring of priorities, costs and progress.

The success of the appointment therefore depends upon the company representative's level of authority in his company and his own understanding of the requirements of the brief. He is the focus of the client's own management of the project, and in all respects is the client in the conventional and well established structure of building design management.

The appointment of a project manager from outside the client's organization is quite different. The managerial skills for which he may be appointed cannot be based upon knowledge of the client's organization sufficient to be of value to the architect in understanding the problem or design needs, or to relieve the architect of any management duties performed by him under the usual terms of appointment.

Unless the project manager can represent the client as a natural extension of his own organization and act with knowledge and the authority of that organization, he is in the same position as the newly appointed architect or consultants. At this early stage these other members of the team have the actual or implied contract obligation to establish direct contact with the client in order to obtain the full briefing which will enable them to proceed with the work. The appointment of an outside project manager by a well intentioned client can have the effect of creating a barrier which actually inhibits access to the right information at the crucial point in the exploratory process. An independent appointment must therefore be conditional upon the ability of the architect to maintain direct access to the client at all times.

The appointment of a client's project manager should not be confused with the statutory need for the appointment of the planning supervisor whose duties are related to matters of health and safety, notification to the Health and Safety Executive, co-ordination and assembly of information in the form of a safety plan to be passed to the principal contractor, and ultimately ensuring that a health and safety file is handed to the client for his own and future occupiers information.

6

Site inspection

Although you may have made yourself familiar with site conditions previously, once formal instruction to proceed with design has been received and a brief discussed, revisit the site making a careful inspection specifically related to the brief. Pending receipt or preparation of accurate survey drawings, sketch notes should be made, the site fully photographed and basic dimensions taken in such a way that this inspection will enable analysis and preliminary design work to begin immediately on sound sources of information relating to, and supplementing, each other.

The information should include:
Site boundaries with approximate dimensions and positions of any existing buildings.
Buildings adjoining or overlooking the site with notes of any windows or openings.
Any features of the site which should be used within the development.
Orientation of the site.
General characteristics of the surrounding landscape, planting, trees and buildings.
Access roads or paths.
Levels on the site and surrounding area, and nature of soil with water table if possible.
Evidence of all services including:
Drains
Water
Electricity
Gas
Telephones
Any failures in specific materials used on existing properties on or near the site.
Names of owners or occupants and postal addresses of surrounding properties.
The local authority, and address, in whose area the property is situated.
General state of the property if an existing building is to be converted.

Consider the site related to its environment. Get away from it far enough to assess its character from all approaches to see how it fits into this environment. See if there are any factors locally that influence the development.

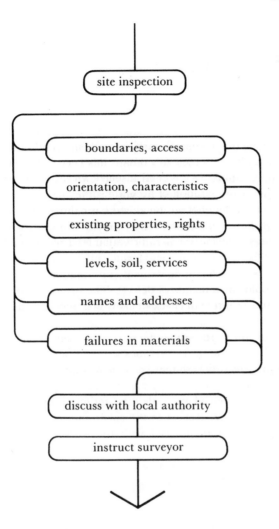

7
Survey

Rather than prepare the true survey yourself, it is in your client's interest to employ the services of a qualified surveyor to prepare this survey. While this is being done, investigate the problem on the basis of your own site inspection notes. The survey should in any case be checked by you on the site.

Where works are to be carried out on existing properties the client should be advised to have a property inspection report prepared, together with measured survey of the premises if this is not already available. These should be prepared by a competent qualified surveyor and also include information as to title, leasehold or tenancy covenants or terms of agreement, information on rights of light or easements and an accurate schedule of defects. The inspection report should be made available to the architect to check items which may have a bearing on the work to be carried out.

If your client asks you to recommend a surveyor, suggest one whose work is known, or, alternatively, ask to see previous survey drawings which have been prepared by them and references so that you can obtain confirmation of accuracy from previous users. Meet the surveyor on the site and explain exactly what is required, including any specific large scale details. Obtain an estimate of cost and time required for the survey. Report to the client and, after approval, instruct the surveyor on his behalf to proceed with the work, giving him letters of introduction.

This is an ideal opportunity to introduce yourself to adjoining owners. Write to them and inform them that the survey is to be carried out and obtain permission to measure any sections of their building which are relevant to the survey requirements.

The survey drawings should be prepared to scales to which you will ultimately prepare your own drawings.

The surveyor should be briefed on the basis of the following check list.

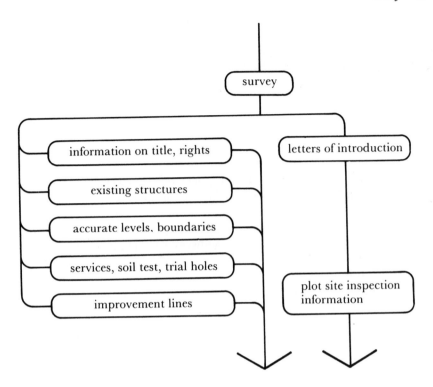

survey

information on title, rights

existing structures

accurate levels, boundaries

services, soil test, trial holes

improvement lines

letters of introduction

plot site inspection information

8
Survey guide

Preliminaries

1   Prepare or have reproduced to appropriate scale a sufficient area of the ordnance survey map to show all boundaries of the site and surrounding or adjoining properties. Check area on geological map, and/or obtain geologist's report. Obtain aerial photographs of the site.

2   Check, and ensure that you have, all necessary equipment.

3   Check with client, solicitor or agent:
Full address of property.
Covenants or other terms in title or lease.
Ownership of fences.
Rights or easements affecting site or adjoining properties.
Age of existing properties and previous occupational uses of either site or buildings.

4   Decide precisely what are the things you will want to learn from the site before going to visit it.

Local authority enquiries

1   Planning or building control considerations, including:
Building or improvement lines.
Future development of area including road or drainage works.
Specific restrictions or conditions governing development.

2   General information on:
Nature of sub-soil and likely bearing capacity, information on local borings.
Water table and liability to flooding.
History of site.
Evidence of any subsidence, erosion or underground workings.
Evidence of material failures peculiar to district.
Main services, including water used for building and positions and depth.
Addresses of public service authorities and preliminary information on existing services.
Obtain forms for the appropriate statutory consents.

Site

1   Orientation and general, natural or other characteristics of site and environment (including overhead).
2   Levels related to bench mark or permanent features.
3   Positions for trial holes, position for spoil during building.
4   Dimensions overall including positions of boundaries, trees (on or adjoining site), buildings, manholes, paths, roads, etc., and general condition.
5   Evidence of all services, drains, inverts and manhole cover levels.
6   Names and addresses of adjoining owners.

Buildings

1   Plans, elevations and sections and selected details, all in sufficient detail for plotting to predetermined scale, adopting running dimensions and with check diagonals to minimize errors.
2   Comprehensive notes on total construction, with sketch details and materials and colour notation in support of measured work including as much hidden foundation work as possible, and tracing and describing all internal and external services, with sizes.
3   Schedule of defects or omitted items with notes on required correction.

Exterior: materials and finishes, including roof, throatings, flashing, weathering, damp course, pointing, ventilators, points of structural failure or horizontal or vertical alignment.

Interior (by room or area, numbered not named): materials and finishes on floors, walls, ceilings and stairs or structural members, and the direction of structural members.

Evidence of rot, beetle, staining, dampness, smell.

Doors and windows: hanging, alignment and opening.

Fittings: alignment, ironmongery.

Services components: electrical, gas
            water
            mechanical
            heating
            ventilation
            fire appliances
            sanitary fittings
            flues and ducts.

4   Comprehensive photographs of site, surroundings and building internally and externally with rule or tape in each photograph, and cross-references to drawn and written information.
5   Description of structural system of the building and specifically in the case of a 'listed' building sufficient information supported by research to ensure that the structural and constructional principles are as well understood as the general details.

9
Briefing process

Briefing is a two-way educational process which takes place between the client and the architect from the beginning. By extended discussion, investigation and analysis of requirements it aims to set up an agreed baseline suitable for secure design development. It must also be recognized as confidential.

It can be a delicate process, through which a client with little knowledge of the method of assembling design data has to be coaxed or directed until he is able to recognize or fulfil the part he needs to contribute in establishing this agreed point of reference. It requires him to take the most detached view of his needs and devote the necessary time to providing the maximum information available.

This can range from discussion, which simply needs to confirm the design attitude towards the small job, to innumerable meetings or visits concerned with teasing out complete information for a large job. In this respect, care needs to be taken in balancing the findings and establishing the relative importance of discussions with different sections of a company in relationship to the views of a board, especially where there appears to be conflict in fact or aspiration.

This information then needs to be considered against the practical conditions within which the design has to be achieved; the information which is obtained from the survey and the factors affecting the development of the site; permissible site coverage, height limitations, boundaries of existing premises, light angles to windows both existing and new, rights or easements established by previous or existing properties, building lines, or future developments nearby. All factors, from bus stops to emergency appliance access, will have their effect upon the options available, and must be considered in the investigation made in support of the proposals to be put forward.

The results represent the essential framework for the design process. They may even suggest that the client's original views need serious reconsideration. The research must be objective if it is to be of value in establishing priorities or in helping to decide between conflicting demands. There are times during design development when the reasons for taking decisions will be questioned: this material should be the dependable background against which to test them.

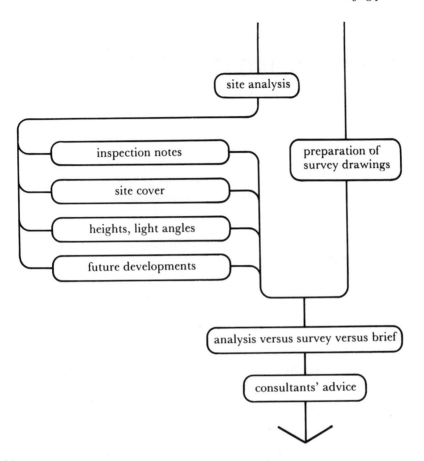

10
Consultant recommendation

On minor works an architect should be able to cope with surveys, estimates, and structural calculations, services, and settlement of final accounts. to attempt to deal with these on a large contract is a mistake. The architect's job under these circumstances is to recommend to the client suitable consultants for the work, to be able to check the work, to be able to work well and simultaneously with the consultant throughout the contract, and to trust and act upon his advice. In its simplest way you, as a person with a working knowledge of the subject, are recommending to the client a man whose specialist knowledge will produce a sounder and more experienced service than the one which you could give. It is best to offer choice from which selection can be made. The decision should be made by the client.

Though you have a co-ordination role for consultants' work it is necessary to establish with your client that your recommendation for specialist services is due to the limitations of your own skills and implicit in this is the need for appointed consultants or specialists to be responsible for their own work.

In recommending consultants, satisfy yourself that they are fully qualified and the best people in all circumstances to do the work. Remember also that where considering utilizing new methods involving an element of risk—even though you may obtain your client's agreement to this—you are obliged to take the best available advice before proceeding. Recommendations for consultancy work should preferably be made from personal knowledge of previous work they have carried out, or the recommendation of a person whose opinion you respect. If your client suggests a consultant who may be unknown to you, satisfy yourself that he fulfils all the conditions you look for in making recommendations of your own.

After making the final selection, discuss the programme and work in general with each, and make your recommendations to the client with all the relevant information on the scale of fees on which the consultants are prepared to carry out the work. Appointment should be made as soon as these are approved by the client. They are 'employed' and paid by the client. They should be appointed directly by him.

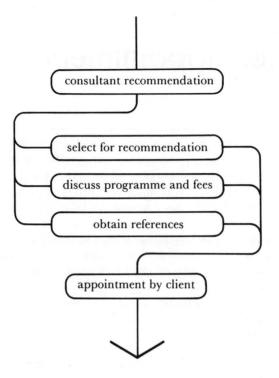

11
Engineer appointment

The client should appoint the engineer direct, although it is not unknown on minor works for a client with little experience to prefer the architect to do this. This should not be confused with provision of an all-in service; the client must remain the employer of the consultant. It is important in this case to have written instructions to do so and that the appointment is confirmed as 'on behalf of the client'. Confirm the terms by letter, including the basis for fees. The engineer's accounts may subsequently be submitted through your own office though will be passed to the client for direct payment. A copy of the letter of appointment should be sent to the client for his records or vice versa when the appointment is made direct.

Arrange an early meeting with the engineer to discuss basic design proposals and include the following points:

1   Soil tests, position of trial holes on the site, and what arrangements should be made for boring these.
2   Materials and general construction relative to the fire and loading classification of the building.
3   Alternative types of structural system within the general conditions and their relationships with mechanical and other services.
4   Relative costs of alternative types of structural systems.
5   Any consents which the engineer should deal with including submission of calculations to local authorities, etc.
6   Deliveries of materials or any special plant, access to site, or site restrictions.
7   His own programme for the work and liaison between his office and yours.

Arrangements should be made at this stage for an illustrated report to be prepared by the engineer to cover these points as necessary, which will accompany the architect's report when submitting design proposals to the client. It should be borne in mind that where one system is being recommended by architect/engineer as most suitable for design or structural reasons, whether lowest cost or not, the principles behind its selection should be made clear in the report.

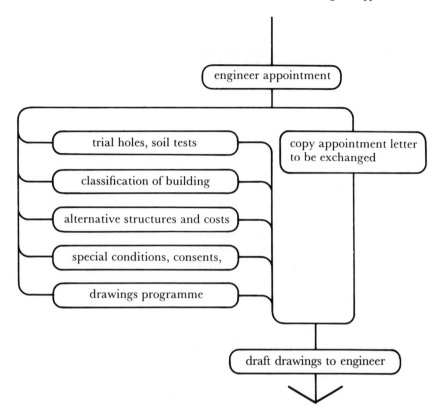

12

Quantity surveyor appointment

The appointment of the quantity surveyor, as with the appointment of the engineer, should be made directly by the client, or perhaps for minor works and only if instructed to do so, by you 'on the client's behalf'. The quantity surveyor is appointed to act on the client's behalf in ultimately keeping the contract under accurate financial control. The quantity surveyor's work is inevitably bound up with the comparison of ways and means. Costs are affected by programmes and contractors' resources as much as initial versus maintenance costs of the building in use. The means by which the quantity surveyor can make the most effective contribution from the outset should be discussed as early as possible.

While taking maximum advantage of cost advice it is necessary to remember that the advice is a guide and not a limit. The client must retain the right to know the architectural options even if more costly, and it should be understood that these must go to the client for decision rather than be blocked by budget allocation.

Discuss these points related to the brief and basic design considerations and arrange for the quantity surveyor to submit a report to accompany your report and design proposals to the client. Your discussions in any event should cover the following:

1 Cost of comparative methods of construction in respect of the current materials and labour costs.
2 The relative merits of different types of contract from a cost control point of view according to the character of work and construction methods under consideration.
3 The time the quantity surveyor will require for the preparation of his bills of quantities, and what form these should take.
4 The date for submission of this document to contractors for competitive tender or an estimate as the basis of a negotiated contract.
5 The time required for negotiation either with the contractor or the client between submission of tender or estimate and placing of contract.
6 The method and period for valuations of works as the site work proceeds and the measurement of variations to the contract.
7 The method of checking daywork, costs and claims on the contract.
8 The means of checking payment by the contractor to sub-contractors on interim certificates.
9 The form for the statement of final account to be agreed with the contractor on behalf of the client.

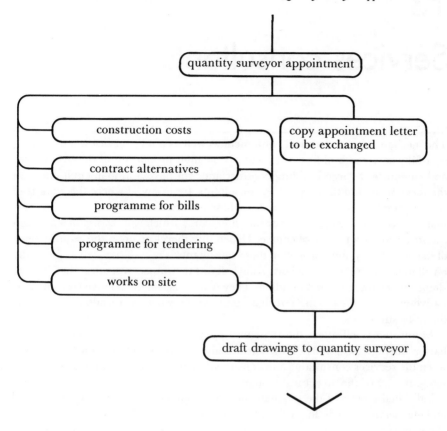

13
Services consultants

The mechanical and electrical equipment as well as public service work involved in a fully serviced building represent a very high proportion of the overall cost and content of a large building contract and will have a fundamental effect on the form of the building. Services consultants are essential where the work is of such a complex nature, but do not let these overlap the technical service of normal sub-contract items for minor building works which will be organized within the structure as a matter of course. Depending therefore upon the requirements of the work, early appointment of these consultants is necessary to advise generally on all items where their specialist knowledge of the subject will affect the ultimate shape and character of the building. They will advise on the relative costs of alternative methods of carrying out these parts of the work in consultation with the quantity surveyors.

Many items will affect the structural systems under consideration and close liaison during discussions on the various alternatives should be maintained between the services consultants and consultant engineer in order that they form an integral part of the structural system.

Individual aspects of the requirements for comprehensive environmental control and the services needs for a building include these listed below and should be carefully considered in the light of your own knowledge and the importance of installations relative to your client's requirements:

Air-conditioning
Heating
Ventilation
Drainage
Hot and cold water services
Electrical installation
Information and communication system
Refuse disposal system
Fire, security and emergency facilities
Vertical transportation lifts/escalators, etc
Other mechanical or specialist services

If you feel that your client would be better served in any or all of these matters by an expert you must make the recommendation as part of your own services.

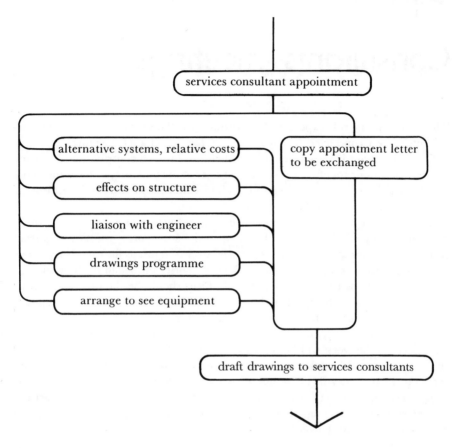

14

Consultants' meetings

The co-ordinating role expected of an architect in relationship to the work of consultants is best conducted by means of regular consultants' meetings.

Each consultant is responsible to the client for his own contribution; his work will have a significant effect upon the character of the building, so these meetings should be held from the very beginning of the commission and continue through to the completion of the final account.

The architect is best suited to convening and acting as chairman for these meetings. They will be attended by the quantity surveyor, consulting engineer, services consultant and the client's representative. And just as the client's representative is expected to have decision-making authority on behalf of the client, so the representatives from the consultants' offices should be the principals, or at very least senior members with authority enabling them to take all the appropriate decisions on behalf of their own practices or companies.

Consultants' meetings become the main design management meetings in which all aspects of the work will be discussed, and at which all members can expect that decisions will be taken and matters resolved by the people attending the meeting. In the early days the matters covered will be programming, briefing, design development, materials and construction method, cost and contract arrangements. The meetings should be held no less frequently than monthly, and during the course of the work on site they will be held as frequently as necessary to ensure immediate attention to current problems. These meetings should not duplicate the work of client's building committee meetings, though are generally complementary in that certain aspects of the two are closely related.

As work proceeds and the construction contract is placed with a contractor, a principal of the contracting firm should be invited to attend consultants' meetings to provide the site aspect of the consultancy team. If the contract is to be placed on the basis of a negotiated price, there is no reason why, conditionally, the contractor should not be asked to attend consultants' meetings in advance of his appointment, in order that any views he has concerning the organization of the site works can be taken into account.

Except for the periodic, and necessarily confidential, financial and overall budget reports submitted by the quantity surveyor to the client independently, the object of consultants' meetings is that all matters including costing should be open to discussion and be resolved as the work proceeds. They are a continuing means of communication between the client, individual consultants and the contractor, and ensures that no problem ever exists for more than the period between meetings, that the contractor is fully aware of the client's needs related to design develop-

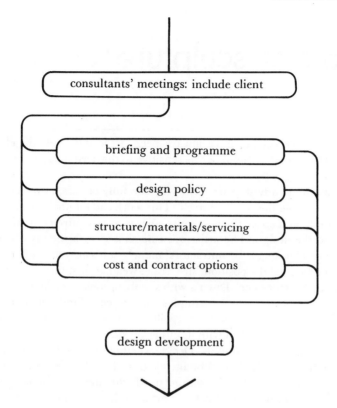

ment and building work, and that the client is kept continuously aware of construction progress, sub-contract co-ordination and any cost and programme changes, while each of the consultants is aware of the effect on his own work of that being done by others.

After construction has begun these meetings must be kept quite separate from site meetings, whose objects are to deal with the day-to-day aspects of site work, and are generally speaking best convened and controlled by the contractor and confined to servicing the domestic needs of the contractor, his sub-contractors and his site.

15
Murals or sculpture

Commissioned works of art have always been associated with the design of buildings and the architect should be as sensitive to the need today as he has been historically.

You have a duty to advise your client very carefully on this, however tempted you may be to handle the work yourself. This work should not be conjured into a building simply as a space filler. It must emerge as a requirement and be fully integrated into the design. The artist must be chosen with the same principles in mind as when choosing sub-contractors, namely suitability for their particular job and bearing in mind the position, size, scale, weathering difficulties, materials, circulation hazards, and so on. Discuss with suitable people samples of their work, or, alternatively, find out where examples can be seen. Find out the materials with which they work best, how long it will take to carry out the commission, how they would propose to deal with it, either on site or in their own studio, and their likely fees, including materials. Decide whether there is any builder's work involved, whether the item should be included in the bill of quantities with the builder's work and treated as a sub-contract or whether the artist should be directly commissioned by the client as a freelance artist and, if so, whether he can make arrangements for site delivery or working in the building. Advise your client, with recommendations, and obtain approval to make the appointment after arranging for him to see samples of the work.

If the cost is being included in the bills of quantities the artist should be warned that this will eventually be paid by the general contractor who will expect him to conform with contract conditions.

Remember that the person you employ will expect to be given a brief quite equal to the brief you would give to the plumbing contractor. This is the point at which you make your own contribution by describing how you think the work should contribute to the building.

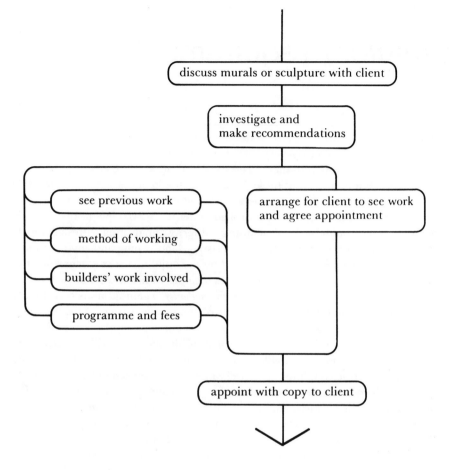

16
Statutory requirements

If there are significant issues to be discussed with the statutory authorities concerning the development options within a particular brief, it is as well to hold preliminary discussions with them to establish attitudes before any serious design work begins. But in any event these discussions should not be deferred later than the sketch proposals stage, when the general nature of the building can be seen.

The standards of building are controlled under three principal headings: *planning*, exercised through the local planning authority and dealing with such things as building use, siting and visual characteristics, landscaping and environmental background; *building regulations*, exercised by the building control department of the local authority and approved inspectors, dealing with construction, safety and health aspects of the building, and the *fire authority;* again administered locally and dealing with the fire prevention, control and escape aspects of the building.

Discussions with the planning officer will give guidance on the scheme in relationship to the local authority structure plan for the area. He will also advise on the procedures and the advisability of making either an outline or a full planning application; historic buildings or conservation area requirements, the views of local amenity societies, the appropriate fees in connection with the application and, for programming purposes, the dates of future planning committee meetings.

Building regulations control offers two routes; either with notice to, or by depositing full plans with, the local authority; or alternatively by appointing an approved inspector who, after serving an initial notice on the local authority jointly with the client, receives acceptance to undertake the full procedure leading to private certification. In the first case a fee is paid to the local authority and in the second to the approved inspector.

Where fire authority approvals are necessary for specific classes of building they will be processed either by the local authority or by the approved inspector as part of the inspection process. Where the case is otherwise or where a fire certificate will be required on completion of the work, it is as well to consult the fire authority independently.

For relatively large scale work any examination requirements will need to be well detailed. Site plans are generally no less than 1:100 scale, general layout or carcass drawings showing overall dimensions and locational reference to other drawings are generally 1:50. Assembly drawings showing specific areas are 1:20, and component drawings covering specific item detailing would be 1:5 or perhaps 1:10. These are the scales which would naturally be adopted for constructional purposes, in any event, so that the work ultimately considered by a certifying or statutory authority will entail detailed working to these scales.

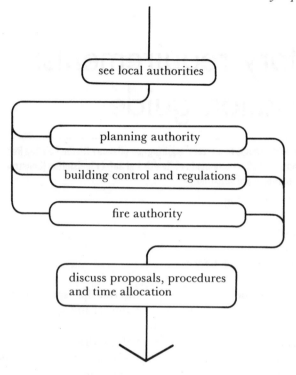

In the circumstances it is important to recognize that the views expressed by the planning authority officers may be more optimistic than those of the planning committee to whom they eventually submit the scheme with recommendations, so any work done in advance of formal confirmation of acceptance by all statutory authorities is, and has to be, speculative in this respect. This is why it is important that work progresses with clear understanding of the statutory requirements, and that the client is made aware of and accepts this situation.

Any formal consents when received should be sent to the client to be deposited with title, but copies should be kept in the office for reference.

In the case of leasehold premises copies of development conditions or restrictions set by the freeholder or owner should be obtained to ensure that the work complies equally with these conditions.

It should be remembered that statutory conditions represent a minimum acceptable condition for the health and safety of occupants. A request to bring proposals into line with requirements, suggests that the work should be looked at also to see whether in the best interests of the client the appropriate architectural standards are being met.

17

Statutory requirements: information guide

These headings provide a guide to matters requiring compliance with the Building Regulations. It is also necessary to ensure that all requirements of Health and Safety legislation (Construction (Design and Management) Regulations) are satisfied.

Materials and workmanship
Structure
    Loading
    Ground movement
    Disproportionate collapse
Fire
    Means of escape   Internal fire spread (structures)
    Internal fire spread (surfaces)   External fire spread
Site preparation and resistance to moisture
    Preparation of site   Subsoil drainage
    Dangerous and offensive   Resistance to weather and ground
      substances   moisture
Toxic substances
    Cavity insulation
Resistance to the passage of sound
    Airborne sound (walls)
    Airborne sound (floors)
    Impact sound (floors)
Ventilation
    Means of ventilation
    Condensation
Hygiene
    Food storage   Hot water storage
    Bathrooms   Sanitary conveniences
Drainage and waste disposal
    Sanitary pipework and drainage   Rainwater drainage
    Cesspools, septic tanks and   Solid waste storage
      settlement tanks
Heat producing appliances
    Air supply
    Discharge of products of combustion
    Protection of building
Stairways, ramps and guards
    Stairways and ramps   Vehicle barriers
    Protection from falling

Conservation of fuel and power
    Resistance to the passage of heat (dwellings)
    Resistance to the passage of heat (buildings other than dwellings)
    Heating system controls
    Insulation of heating services
Facilities for disabled people

A planning application submitted through the appropriate local planning authority will require to satisfy the following points:

Full address or location of site/property
Certificate of notice to owners where not the applicant
Name and address of applicant/owner
Type of development (new, conversion including demolition, or change of use
Whether outline or full consent is required
Present use of site
Access to highway (new, existing, or modified)
Whether permanent or limited life development
Description of external materials and colour
All information relative to industrial or commercial use
Areas—vehicle parking, loading, etc.
Drawings, showing development to 1:100
Drawing showing location plan related to existing buildings, trees and roads

Consider possible need for subsidiary consents:

Listed building
    Where an independent application for listed building consent is
    required, or the need to check status in conservation areas.
Landlord or lessor
    Where conditions of lease will affect planning, construction, work on
    site, or reinstatement
Insurance company
    Where terms of insurance are likely to be affected or special
    precautions necessary to comply with terms
Adjoining owners
    Where works are likely to affect walls or structure jointly owned
    under the terms of the London Building Acts, or where other rights
    are held over the site or property
Main architect
    Where works are on a tenancy in a building still under construction
Royal Fine Art Commission
    Where design affects public amenity, work to be carried out under
    financial grant to local authority or otherwise client or local authority
    want guidance from RFAC.

18
Design proposals

Drawings should be prepared in basic form to illustrate the principles of the design sufficiently, including external works, landscaping, etc., to enable intelligent discussion with:
1 Client
2 Quantity surveyor
3 Consultants
4 Sub-contractors

They should be prepared with a view to being developed for the establishment of necessary approvals when agreed by the client. Clients either want to go into every detail, or get it all over quickly on the assumption that you will deal with everything on their behalf. It is essential, therefore, that the scheme you present is one about which you feel fully confident from a design and technical point of view. It must always fulfil these conditions and, if not, you should delay presentation and inform the client accordingly.

Drawings should be to scale with general dimensions only. They should be a clean statement, easily read by a layman unfamiliar with drawings, but taken to a point where the architect can demonstrate the scheme in considerable detail to the client. Because many people find plans, sections and elevations difficult to understand, this must be taken into account in the presentation material.

Before presentation:
(a) discuss proposals with consultants and specialists to check any points on which you have any doubt;
(b) if necessary check proposals again with local authorities;
(c) prepare illustrative drawings and/or a supporting model;
(d) prepare a collection of material samples or illustrations and check beforehand that these will be available for use when required;
(e) prepare a concise report which should be supported by and read with reports from consultants and quantity surveyor.

This collection should represent firm design proposals based on consideration of the different possibilities. Solutions which have been discarded during investigation can be referred to, or be available, but only to justify the scheme put forward, and not as alternatives.

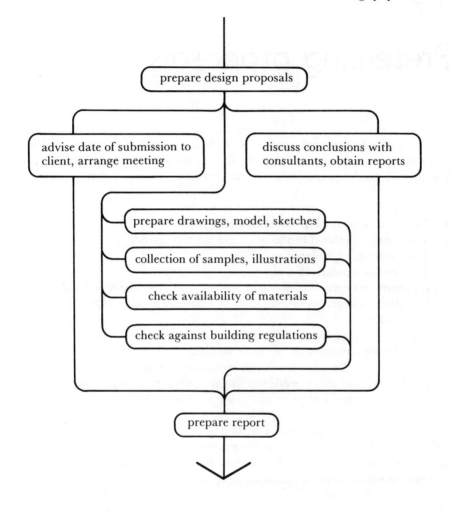

19

Presenting proposals

Design proposals, when submitted to your client, will include a report and assessment of costs for the work. There should be enough copies to provide for each member where the proposals are being considered by a committee.

The report should state clearly and concisely:
1 The client's original terms of reference/brief.
2 Your analysis related to the brief and the site conditions.
3 Your attitude to different possibilities.
4 Your recommendations and why.
5 An approximate assessment of cost, including all professional fees and expenses (anticipating expenses in settlement of adjoining owners' rights, etc., where applicable).
6 An assessment of the period required for detailed development of the design work before construction can start on site.
7 A request for the adoption of the recommendations and for instructions to proceed in detail with a gentle warning that acceptance means second thoughts on the brief after this point can cause serious disruption.

Unless the client is specifying a particular date as necessary for occupation of the building the assessment of the construction period is best left to the contractor(s) as this can have a significant effect on the cost of the building.

The information from the quantity surveyor, engineer or other consultants will be complementary, but ideally independent documents to this report, and all should be carefully cross-referenced to the design drawings. It is important to establish in the client's mind—and perhaps even some consultants'—the independent nature of consultants' advice.

Their contributions can only be made fully where they take—and must be seen to be taking—direct responsibility for views expressed and actions they propose.

For contracts on which a quantity surveyor or consultants are not employed, the assessment of building costs, as well as being calculated on a superficial area, should be cross-checked by the same methods on contracts which are directly comparable, recently finished and on which completed contract costs are known (preferably on a building in the same locality).

If you are suggesting new forms of construction, your client must be informed of any potential risks involved. In doing this it does not relieve you of your responsibility to obtain the best available advice on the techniques concerned. Though

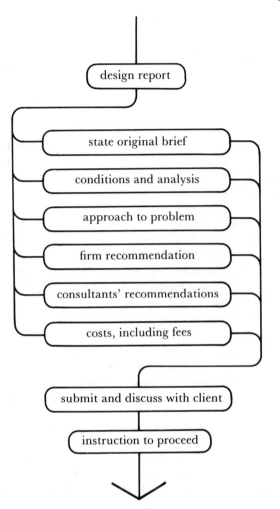

it is often suggested that reports should be sent in advance of meeting, it is best avoided. It is better to arrange a meeting with your client at which these proposals can be presented and discussed fully and the recommendations amplified as necessary by you. A further meeting for questions can be held if time is needed to consider the proposals.

20
Interim fees

With a large scheme an interim fee may have been submitted at outline proposal stage or following submission of preliminary feasibility studies, but it is as likely to have been held over until the submission of the design proposals at this scheme design stage where the work is not too extensive.

The account will be submitted in accordance with the fee arrangement agreed in the terms of appointment. It should list the stages through which the work has passed up to the point at which the work is ready to proceed to contract stage. Where charged as a percentage of the contract cost the fee will be based on the provisional assessment of building cost as submitted in the report, but it should be noted on the account that the final fee will be adjusted on the basis of the final contract figure on completion of the works.

Reimbursable expenses should be claimed on the account for costs involved beyond those which are regarded as included in the fee and the date up to which these have been incurred should be noted on the account. On a large contract incurring heavy travelling or similar expenses, there is no reason why the expense accounts should not be submitted at regular intervals such as monthly or quarterly even if the fees for professional services are submitted at pre-determined stages of the work.

In the absence of more sophisticated office/job accounting systems, it is advisable, for office records, to attach cost analyses of principals' and assistants' time, including overheads, to the office copy of this account. These serve as reference for time-charge assessments where estimates of likely fees are requested by a client in advance of commissioning work or, alternatively, to give an analysis of work throughout the office in terms of staff costs for different types of work, and for arranging contract programmes and salary scales generally.

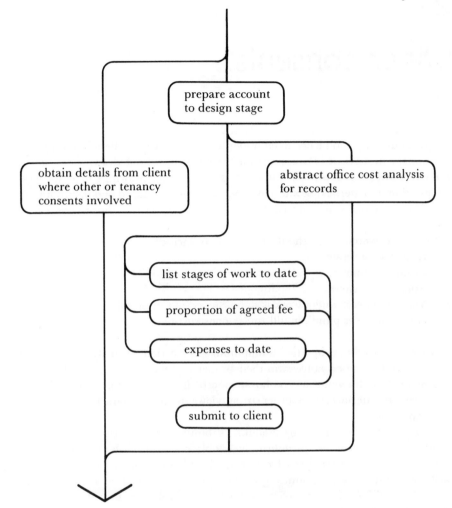

21
Other consents

Where a building is to be occupied under lease and once the client has approved preliminary designs, it is necessary for the client to submit drawings to all interested parties for approval. These should be design drawings together with specification of materials, or alternatively, drawings developed and incorporating specification notes equivalent to those submitted for local authority consents.

The list to whom these should be sent may include:
(a) Landlord or lessor
(b) Insurance company
(c) Adjoining owners
(d) Main architect: where work is to be carried out in premises which are part only of a main building still under construction.

Where Estates own properties, a minimum specification is usually insisted upon for works to be carried out within their properties and a copy of this should be obtained before drawings are too far advanced. Estates may insist upon the use of particular materials and express strong views upon the character of the work to be approved.

Drawings showing proposals should be submitted to the client for him to circulate to those concerned, or alternatively obtain a list from him so that copies of the drawings can be sent to each direct. Find out how many copies of the drawing each will require before submitting applications for approval, as subsequent requests for additional copies prolong negotiations. Owner's approvals, comments or requests for modification must be reported to the client in order that the leasehold terms can be set out, checked, or revised by the respective solicitors.

If your client or the local authority require the views of the Royal Fine Art Commission, this is the best stage at which to get their guidance.

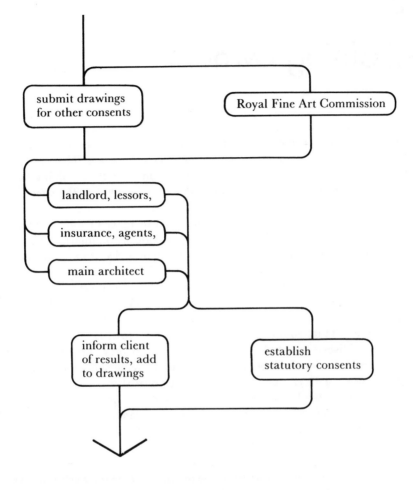

22

Adjoining owners

From the site analysis it should be evident what rights or easements an adjoining owner could justifiably claim to enjoy over your site or building. There is a legal obligation to respect these or otherwise come to terms with the adjoining owner in settlement of them. Consideration must therefore be given to the effect your building will have on the rights of light, air, access, support, drainage or other essential services to his building. Enquiries should be made of your client as to any restrictions over the land, but do not rely uncritically on information given by third parties and, if necessary, insist on written advice from your client's solicitor.

With any project it is necessary to establish ownership of walls and precise boundaries. Inspect plans attached to title deeds. Check whether earlier party agreements have been made.

Bearing in mind that your client may wish to make use of similar rights which have been established by a building which exists on or previously occupied his own site, each condition must be satisfied by mutual agreement or settlement at this stage, as oversight can be very expensive to rectify.

Outside London work may not cross a boundary. An agreement with a neighbour must cover the extent of the construction related to the boundary, access and responsibility for maintenance, access for works and indemnity against damage. The agreement should be signed by both owners.

In London, where proposals include works to a wall, foundations, or parts of the structure which are jointly owned by the building owner and adjoining owner the precise boundary should be established and statutory regulations complied with in respect of the service of notice of intention to carry out the works according to the type of work. In London, or outside, it is advisable to agree a schedule of condition of adjoining premises before starting work.

These regulations set out specifically by definition the appropriate categories of *party* or joint-ownership, the rights enjoyed by each owner to carry out works to the structure, the financial settlement or respective liabilities in each category, and the conditions under which notice must be served on an adjoining owner or owners. In any event, inform the adjoining owner of intended works even if notice is not required. As works must always comply with the regulations governing construction related to party structures, discuss proposals with the controlling local authority before serving notices, or settling minor works with adjoining owners.

Before embarking on any party wall or joint-ownership negotiations, read the appropriate regulations.

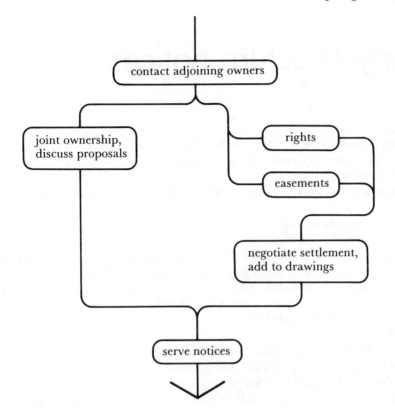

23

Party structure notices

Works to a party structure require the service of formal notice to the adjoining owners and drawings showing the proposed work should be prepared to accompany the notices.

The RIBA have formal notices dealing with each of the categories of works to jointly-owned property:

Form A—Party Structures.

Form B—Party Fence Walls.

Form C—Intention to build within ten feet and at a lower level than the bottom of the foundations of Adjoining Owner's Building.

Form D—Intention to build within twenty feet of the Adjoining Owner's independent building and to a depth as defined.

Form E—Party Walls and Party Fence Walls on line of junction of adjoining lands.

Form F—Walls or Fence Walls on Building Owner's land with footings and foundations projecting into Adjoining Owner's land.

Form G—Selection of Third Surveyor.

Each form sets out the general terms and conditions of the relative parts of the regulations for the information of the person on whom it is served. The sections specifically relating to the works and a description of the works are to be entered on the form to suit the particular case.

Adjoining owners include all those with a lease of more than twelve months and each of these must independently have notice. These should be served allowing the specified time before it is intended to start work—e.g., a party structure notice should allow two months before work is to begin. On receipt of notice each adjoining owner has the right to:

(a) Serve a counter notice relating to his own requirements with full descriptions and drawings for which work he must pay. This must be served within the specified time and the building owner must comply unless the works requested are injurious or cause delay or he dissents by not replying within fourteen days.

(b) Agree in writing within fourteen days from the service of the party structure notice.

(c) Dissent by not writing within fourteen days from service of the notice, after which a difference is established and he must appoint a surveyor to act for him.

The party structure notice is not effective unless work to which it relates is started within six months from date of notice.

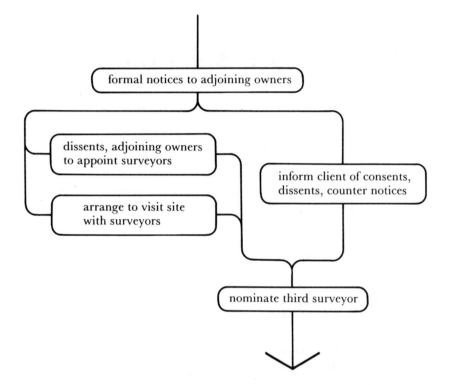

24

Party structure settlement

Dissent to a party structure notice is established by an adjoining owner not consenting in writing to the works described in the notice within fourteen days. After that time the adjoining owner must either:

(a) Agree to use the same surveyor as the building owner to settle the difference—known as the 'Agreed Surveyor'.

(b) Nominate his own surveyor.

Where he nominates his own surveyor the two surveyors must nominate a third surveyor.

The following points are to be borne in mind during negotiations:

1 The adjoining owner has ten days after written request to appoint his surveyor. Failure to do so gives the building owner's surveyor the right to proceed as an agreed surveyor.

2 Either surveyor must act within ten days of written request to select a third surveyor, or an officer of the local authority, as defined by the regulations, may act on application from the other surveyor in selecting the third surveyor.

3 If a third surveyor does not act within ten days of written request another third surveyor may be selected by the other two.

4 All appointments must be made in writing

5 The agreed surveyor, or any two surveyors shall settle by award any dispute relative to the party structure notice.

6 The third surveyor makes the award if no two are able to agree within fourteen days of a request to do so.

7 The award shall be conclusive and shall include the costs incurred for the works and the award as decided by the surveyor or surveyors.

8 There is the right of appeal to the County Court against the award within fourteen days of its delivery.

The draft award of description of work and drawing are prepared by the building owner's surveyor and exchanged with the adjoining owner's surveyor until agreed, after which the final documents are exchanged and each deposited with the respective owners to become part of title. Keep your client informed.

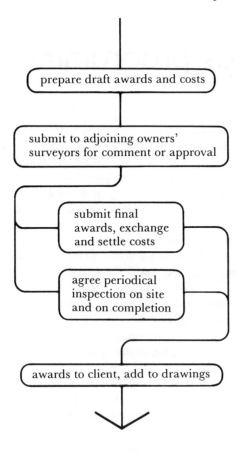

25
Drawings programme

Drawings, from this point forward, in searching out and finding design answers to every detail of the building, are prepared for the sole purpose ultimately of conveying information to the people concerned with constructing the building. It is important, therefore, that you base them upon and relate them to accurate survey drawings; that you follow a well pre-planned system of setting down the information and that the system you adopt will do everything to avoid ambiguity in interpretation. The scales generally adopted are 1:50 for the general layout, carcass, information with dimensional grids and references to other drawings; 1:20 for assembly and area detailing, and 1:5 for large scale, component, detailing. The scales should be agreed with consultants as equally suited to their work. With the reprographic options to enlarge or reduce drawn details it is as well to include graphic scales on all drawings.

In principle the drawings programme should follow a pattern which absorbs consultants' and other information at the right stage to avoid constant repetition and modification.

1 The drawings should be developed to a stage where they carry as much general information as is necessary to establish early consents. It is in this stage that:
   (a) Calculations are made for thermal and sound insulation, heating, ventilation and light.
   (b) They are exchanged with engineers and other consultants for layouts of respective requirements.
   (c) They absorb from public service departments information on existing and suggested new services.
   (d) They form the basis of discussion with representatives for general trade enquiries on sub-contract or supplier's work.
2 The second stage, which should run concurrently with the calculations, discussions and enquiries, is the preparation of draft details and schedules based on the analysis of incoming information and the materials and construction methods under consideration. You must work in constant liaison with your consultants on this. Where the work is suited to phased handover to the quantity surveyor for billing, the order of drawings is of considerable importance to the quantity surveyor's programme, he should therefore be consulted early.
3 The final stage is when all information is brought together to form one comprehensive set of construction drawings from which quantities will be taken and the work carried out on site.

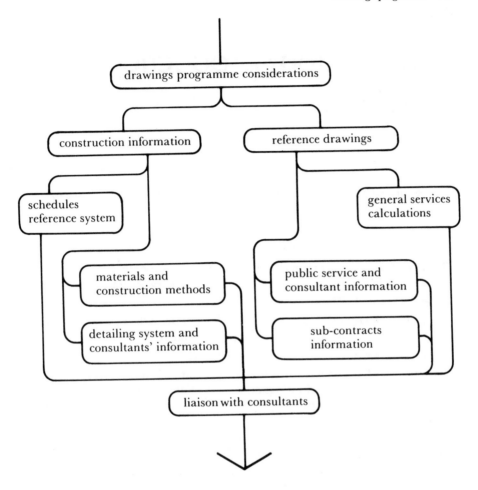

During the preparation of all drawings and information, there is the need to be aware of and minimize all risk, or otherwise to identify any likely hazard related to health and safety. This should be recorded as information for the safety plan and to be incorporated in a final health and safety file to be passed to the client on completion of the work.

With manually prepared drawings, beware of the hypnosis of unnecessary miles of brickwork hatching and timber graining. The joiners' shop always redraws the full size details anyway, and the meticulously drawn small scale information is always illegible on a wet building site. Remember also, when trying to convey information, that both you and the contractor learned construction by isometric or similar illustration.

26

Construction/production drawings

General layout drawings: this reference information should be built up with the following points in mind:

1 They are not details of construction but reference drawings to supporting information which will be in the form of details, schedules, or bills of quantities.

2 They should show only dimensions sufficient to prepare the site, to set out the building in carcass form, and read as complementary documents to layouts prepared by consultants.

3 They should give written general information related to the carcass only, but where services consultants are not supplying separate service layout drawings, they should show main service runs.

4 Their primary function is to carry accurate and comprehensive cross-references to details, other people's drawings and all scheduled items. The scale should be chosen accordingly (generally 1:50).

Construction details: which in the first instance are prepared in draft form as your own investigation drawings, will probably cover all of the building exhaustively. As such, they should be produced quickly for early exchange with consultants and can be frankly 'rough,' marked 'rough,' and to scales which will ultimately be sensible for all details (probably 1:20 and 1:5). 'Exhaustively' means that the details should be investigated three-dimensionally and by 'exploded' view as well as to scale if junctions are to be fully appreciated visually and constructionally – this includes services as well as solving architraves hard against a partition. Draft schedules should run concurrently in order to assess the construction implications.

Contract drawings: are all these items developed to represent a statement of agreed information (including your party settlement agreements) which can be passed to the quantity surveyor and finally issued to the contractor. They should be the minimum number of drawings which give all production information. They will have picked up all the relevant information from consultants and transferred to scale the agreed, exchanged, details and will exploit the value of the three-dimensional sketches. Since all this information is inevitably read together by the client, the estimator and the site agent, on a small scale job there is a strong argument in favour of associating schedules and the construction details with the key drawings whenever possible.

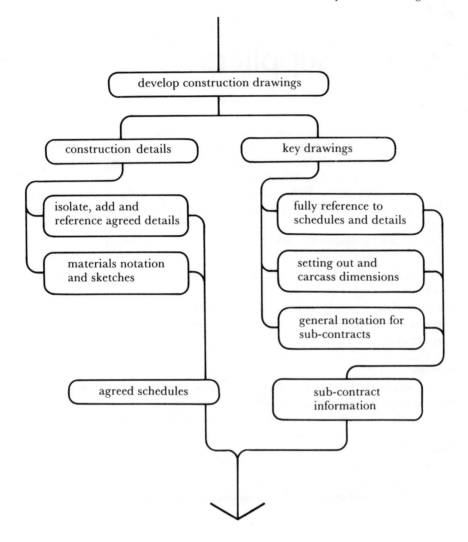

27

Services suppliers

As soon as the general reference layout drawings have reached a sufficiently detailed stage to explain proposals, they should be discussed with, or copies sent to, the appropriate services supplier. Information on those services which exist on the site can then be plotted on the drawings and the authority can make recommendations and submit estimates (three copies for later distribution) for extending the service to the new property.

You will need to discuss the following with the various suppliers:

Water

Size, materials, depth, position and pressure of existing service; meter pit requirements and materials; water storage requirements or other recommendations; arrangements which can be made for builder's supply.

Drainage

Size, materials and invert levels of existing drains; positions at which storm-water drain and soil drains can be entered and, where applicable, recommendations on materials and construction other than the byelaw minimum.

Electricity

Capacity, protective material, position and/or depth of existing service, metering arrangements and types of service required.

Transformer positions, possible amendment or resiting requirements.

Gas

Size, material, depth and position of existing service; metering requirements.

Telecommunications

Position and/or depth of existing services and recommendations on installation and siting of equipment.

Fire Service

In development of earlier discussions and in conjunction with water services, recommendations on dry risers—sizes and pressures—type of equipment, valves and access, etc., and suggested positions for lightning conductors. The information required from each should also include any regulations on fittings, rates,

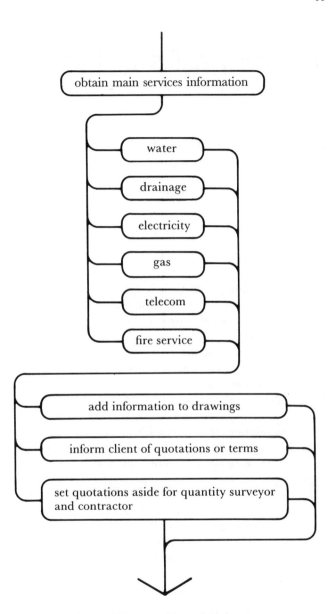

maintenance accessibility and suggested duct sizes, the division of costs for the works, the amount of builder's work required for the service with the description for inclusion in the bills of quantities; what notice is required for commencement of works, how long it will take to complete the work; arrangements for testing on completion and any other relevant information.

28
Environmental services

While dealing with services supply enquiries, other services requirements for the building which may need to be investigated are:

Heating
Ventilation
Water services and drainage
Mechanical services
Electrical installation
Specialist equipment

This is done in relationship with the selection of materials and the basic decisions on service facilities which are thought to be best suited to meet performance requirements. It can only be done by calculating:

Air change requirements
Heat losses and thermal insulation
Airborne and structure-borne sound transmission, insulation and acoustics
Daylight levels and penetration
Artificial light levels

The various solutions must then be considered and alternatives measured practically, financially, and visually against the requirements emerging from each calculation. It must be remembered throughout these investigations that one service often reacts against another, and a superficially economical installation for one service may mean disproportionately high maintenance or running costs for another, or even much more builder's work which is not immediately evident from the calculation and solution alone. Decisions can only be taken after alternatives have been considered individually and collectively in terms of:

(a) Installation versus running or maintenance costs.
(b) Builder's work and/or attendance.
(c) Planning requirements, plant space, trunking, ducts, access, etc.
(d) Byelaw compliance, fire precautions, security and insurance.

A consultant will probably have been employed for a complex installation, but it is still essential that your own analysis is made beforehand to ensure that your discussions with the consultant are based upon a set of requirements which are known to you, and that the results will be correctly related to those on which specialist services are not required and for which you will be responsible.

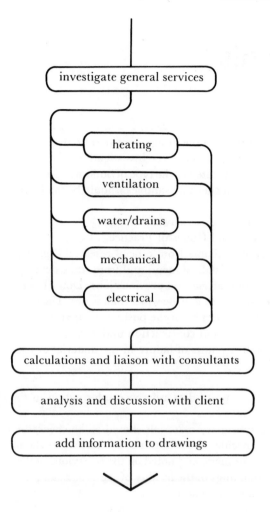

29

Materials

Running concurrently with the design considerations in respect of general planning, there should be an exhaustive investigation of alternative materials and methods of construction suited to the type of building. Careful analysis of all data, including obtaining and checking samples, should be made with special reference to:

1 Building regulations or byelaws.
2 British Standards and Codes of Practice.
3 The information available from official research organizations, such as the Building Research Establishment, and from trade development associations.
4 The behaviour of materials on previous jobs. Don't hesitate to contact other offices whose experience may be wider than yours. The local authority building control officer will often be in the position to advise you on the performance of specific materials and construction under local conditions. It is more important to note the points of failure in the material or construction than the merits.

The importance of up-to-date reference information in the office cannot be overstated.

Structural and subsidiary materials should all be checked for weathering and exposure on the particular site. Short lists of alternatives should be prepared and accurate observations made and noted on the behaviour of these materials where used on existing buildings in the locality of the site. Examples should be examined for weakness taking into account orientation of the material on the building, the degree of exposure and any other influence (whether under trees, etc.). A check against adverse chemical reaction should also be made of materials which may be used together, and, internally as well as externally, consideration should be given to pattern staining or other defects which may arise.

The final assessment must be made only after you, with your quantity surveyor, have prepared an equally accurate analysis of initial costs against maintenance costs, etc., in order that recommendations to clients will give fully substantiated and unbiased information and allow them the opportunity to select or approve a material knowing the full facts behind its choice.

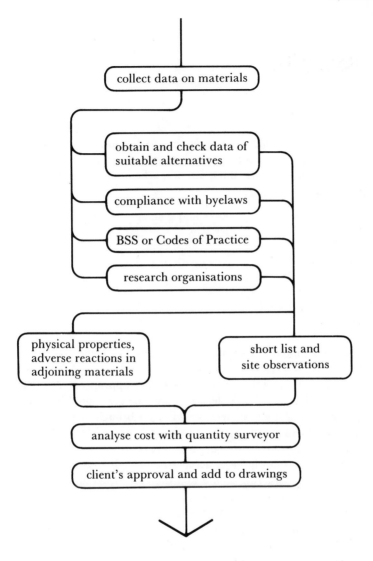

30
Schedules

Recurring contract items should be set out in schedule form with each item described and cross-referenced on the appropriate drawing to the position it is to take in the building. Those items which are best scheduled to prevent confusion on drawings include:

Doors ⎫
Windows ⎬ incorporating lintels and glazing
⎭
Ironmongery
Sanitary fittings
Joinery and fittings
Electrical fittings
Finishes and decorations
Furnishings

The schedules should be prepared concurrently with the construction drawings and, while in the preliminary stages, should be discussed fully with the client. It is important that schedules are read with their appropriate key drawings, as it is at this stage that the client's decisions must be given on things he may have overlooked. Extended briefing meetings will have brought out a great deal of this information but there are always many domestic items which cannot always be anticipated and may range through such things as:

Key systems and possibly locks acceptable to their insurers.
Types of glass, considering sound and thermal insulation.
Cleaners' sinks, drinking water points, etc.
Joinery finishes, locks on cupboards, adjustable shelving.
Switching systems and metering.
Surface finishes related to the use of particular areas.
Accommodation of existing and the extent of new furnishing.

The schedules include items in daily use and will in many cases be the things on which your client has positive views. Samples and illustrations with alternatives, and with an analysis prepared in conjunction with the quantity surveyor of relative costs, should all be available for discussion and be set in accurately comparable form. Everything needing your client's approval must be anticipated and decided upon now, as many of the construction details being prepared in conjunction with these items are dependent upon these being agreed at this stage.

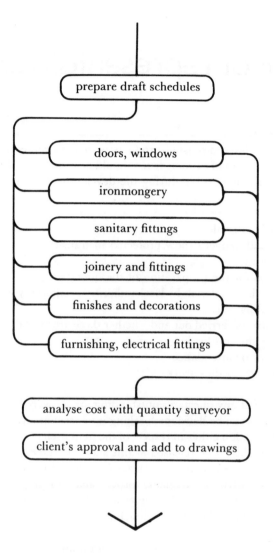

31
Technical representatives

Although you may have discussed products with sales representatives earlier, technical representatives of suitable firms should be called in to discuss materials or products as early as possible during the development of drawings.

The proposals should be discussed in respect of:
(a) Suitability of materials.
(b) Availability and delivery (how protected in transit).
(c) Terms of contract.
(d) Time required for the preparation of the quotation.
(e) Acceptance of their materials by local authorities, conformity with British Standards, fire rating, etc.
(f) Previous contracts carried out and whether these are available for inspection.
(g) Access to the site (off-loading arrangements).
(h) Builder's work or attendance.
(i) Tolerance to which they work.

It is important that any questions outstanding are answered at these meetings so that the drawings can be developed, taking into account anything which is affected by the information either in respect of the item itself or other works related to it. No drawings should be released at this stage. Formal invitation to tender for works should not be issued at this stage but should be held until drawings are complete. It is inadvisable to release 'provisional' drawings as subsequent enquiries and developments may necessitate modification, and it can lead to the wrong drawing reaching the site or workshop if that firm is eventually chosen to carry out the work.

It is at this point that the design is often compromised and the basic concept lost in adjusting details to overcome technical problems. Before accepting modification you must be very sure, therefore, that a technical 'impossibility' is not merely 'more difficult'. If a technical difficulty is a real one and likely to affect the general character of things, the design should be reconsidered to bring it into conformity with the basic principles.

Refer back to the design report from time to time to remind yourself of the principles outlined to the client. These are easily forgotten in overcoming problems.

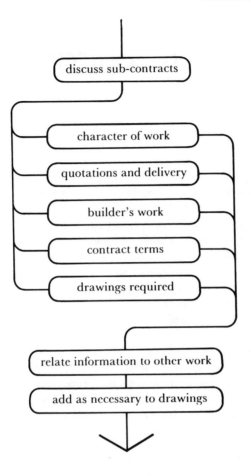

32

Construction contract

Before inviting estimates from sub-contracting companies, it will be necessary to take some firm decisions on the nature of the contract to be used between the client and the main contractor; that is, the printed form setting out the articles of agreement and procedures for conducting the construction operations on the site.

The most generally used form in the industry is that which has evolved over many years and through different revisions, under the hands of the Joint Contracts Tribunal, a body representing all aspects of the consultancy professions, and construction industry. Because the terms in these publications are accepted as fairly balanced by the institutions representing the various facets of the construction industry, they are generally regarded as a legally sound way of placing a contract with a general contractor for any construction work, and the one to which the RIBA gives its agreement through its own membership of the Joint Contracts Tribunal.

It is not the only contract suitable for construction work, as there are forms published by other architectural and allied bodies as well as those which have their emphases towards engineering work, landscape work or interior design work. The choice of form depends entirely upon the nature of the work in hand, and indeed the views of the client, legal adviser or other members of the consultancy team.

The standard JCT form is known as a lump sum contract in which, under the usual procedures, a contractor having submitted a tender in competition with other contractors, gives a total price for the work which is entered in the articles of agreement as a lump sum.

The two basic variations of this standard form are one for use with bills of quantities and another for use without bills of quantities, but the range of forms includes versions for private or local authority use and other variations which also deal with different sizes of job. Most forms also include their own supporting range of documents related to the conditions and procedures required of the selected form.

The importance of deciding the type of contract to be used at this stage is that a potential sub-contracting company must be aware of the conditions under which the contract will be carried out on site, and the terms under which they will be expected to undertake their work in relationship to the main contract. They must also know whether they will be required to undertake responsibility for a design element of their work by means of an independent agreement with the client. It is equally important for all members of the team to know how these sub-trades are to fit into the construction pattern, and whether at this stage of the work they will be entitled to ask companies to provide detailed drawings or calculations for work.

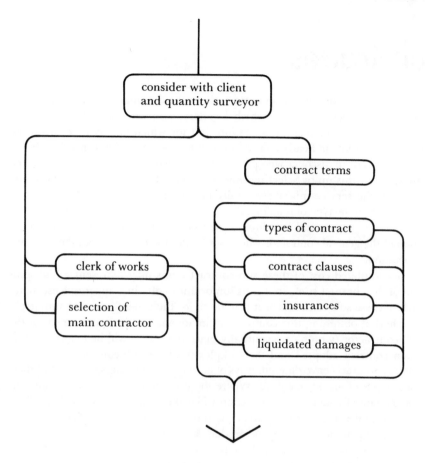

33
Sub-trades

Sub-trades will require attention quite early in the development of design work. These are the trades or services which a general contractor would not normally supply from within his own organization, but for which the architect will need detailed information and early consultation with sub-contracting firms. In the first instance he needs to discover who provides the type of service or equipment, and will then follow this up by selecting those who would be best suited to do so and from whom the service might eventually be obtained.

Depending upon the type of building, the number of these potential sub-contractors can be quite extensive, and in a lump sum contract they will all come under the direction of the general contractor who co-ordinates their services into the construction operation.

The accumulated cost of these sub-contract items may represent a high proportion of the contract sum, so it is as important to obtain competitive estimates for each of these sub-contracts as it is to do so for the general contract sum itself. The method of obtaining this competition in advance of the appointment of the general contractor (who must eventually place the order) will be determined by the main contract adopted and the complexity of the sub-contract.

Different contracts have different ways of accommodating this situation, but there are three types of arrangement: (a) Where there are any number from whom the contractor himself could make a selection when the contract is placed, (b) Where there are a limited number who would be suited to it, but with similar service or products, (c) Where there is a specific product, and only one firm that could possible handle the sub-contract; or where there is a long manufacturing period.

When it is evident from the drawings which parts of the work will require sub-contract services, each item can be considered in the light of the following:

1 It may be possible from information given in trade literature or by technical representatives to draw and describe the work sufficiently for it to be measured in the usual way by the quantity surveyor, for inclusion in the bills or described in the specification. It will then be absorbed into the general contract. This is by far the least complicated in contract terms. The contractor will seek competition from his own selected firms and will ultimately obtain your approval to sub-let the work to his own successful sub-contractor as a domestic sub-contractor. The general contractor becomes responsible for the work and no special contract arrangements have to be made.

2 Where it is evident from your drawings that there are a number of firms who could provide the services required, and apart from price there is little to choose between the level of service or type of product which each can provide, it is possible for you to prepare drawings which can accommodate the services of the selected sub-contractor later and to include in documents for the general contractor a list of suitable firms from which he is entitled to invite competitive tenders and make his own selection. These again become domestic sub-contractors, for whom he becomes responsible.

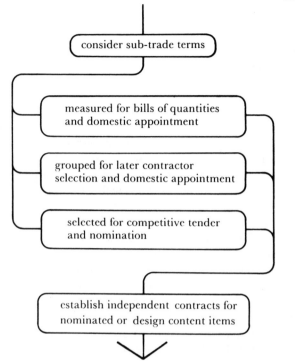

consider sub-trade terms

measured for bills of quantities and domestic appointment

grouped for later contractor selection and domestic appointment

selected for competitive tender and nomination

establish independent contracts for nominated or design content items

3 When the sub-contract work will need the close attention and collaboration of a specialist firm during the preparation of drawings, it will require nomination of the company in advance of the general contractor's appointment. In the normal type of building contract advance nomination requires an independent agreement between the sub-contractor and the client, which will follow the terms of the main contract to be adopted.

4 Where the sub-contract work includes a design element provided by and associated with the performance of the service in any of these situations, it is necessary for an agreement between sub-contractor and client to recognize this, with a consideration for the design content.

In any of the cases where a sub-contract operation is not being measured in the bills or described in the specification as part of the building contract, financial provision for the work is made in the form of a prime cost or provisional sum. This is assessed in advance and included in the bills of quantities as a sum set aside to cover the cost of the sub-contract operation and associated builder's work or attendance. This sum is reconciled in the final account against the final cost of the work.

A second and similar category of independent sub-trade is that covering the supply of items which the contractor instals on site. All the foregoing points apply equally to supply items. They can be specified and measured, listed, or nominated in advance where supplying very particular articles or those with long delivery dates, and a prime cost sum can be set aside in the bills, against which the supplied item will be balanced in the final account.

34

Practice

Practising a profession has been described as offering an authoritative and dependable service to the extent of one's personal estate in exchange for a fee. The background against which the law entitles a profession to be practised will change from time to time, but the underlying need will always call for this level of commitment. In return for this total commitment to a profession it was necessary to stand outside commercial competition and accept institutional conditions of engagement aimed at offering a client a level of service and expertise from any equally qualified practitioner on a set scale of professional charges. Now, outside those conditions, but within the traditional level of responsibility demanded by law of practising architects, that commitment becomes all the more difficult to demonstrate and the need to do so the more important.

The need for identifiable professionalism in the handling of the client's affairs will always be an important element of architectural practice. The sums an architect spends on behalf of his client, the recommendation of other people's services and the advice he gives about manufacturing and construction industries; all require the most serious attention. It must be clear that any action taken or advice given is totally impartial and uninfluenced by anything except knowledge and experience. This is particularly important where, by tradition, fees for professional services have been expressed as a percentage of the final contract cost of the building work, even though the object of competitive tendering for both sub-contract work and the main construction operation is to provide the most economical building within those terms.

Nevertheless it follows that great care must be taken to ensure that the client recognizes the impartiality with which materials and companies are selected and recommended, and the position should never be prejudiced by allowing conditions which could be seen to influence judgment by favour or incentive.

The law recognizes the unique semi-arbitrator position which the architect occupies under the traditional forms of contract generally adopted for building operations. It has been said that this privileged position was gained by architects having demonstrated that they could be trusted to perform the role with impartiality, and that they retain it with the construction industry's acceptance.

It can be seen therefore that from both the client's and a contractor's point of view the architect must be seen to tread a scrupulously fair path in the conduct of the business; from the client's viewpoint because the entire basis of his fee is related to the cost of the building operation, and from the contractor's point of view because the architect is commissioned and paid by the client, but is expected to take impartial decisions in his interpretation of the contract.

35
Sub-contract tenders

When the contract can be seen on the drawing board in construction stages or trades and where work cannot be measured in the bills of quantities or be the subject of domestic sub-contracts, decisions should be taken on which items are to be dealt with as:

(a) Work for which materials are to be supplied and delivered and which will be carried out on the site entirely by the sub-contractor; a sub-contract item.

(b) Work for which materials or items of equipment are to be supplied and delivered only and fixed on the site by the general contractor; a supply item.

Unless requiring a specific service or specific materials, each can be the subject of competitive tender. Having first investigated the potentialities and suitability of a product or firm with the technical representatives, a full list of the firms you propose to approach should be compiled and sent to the client for final approval. It is also necessary to advise the client of any independent agreements which may be required.

Any additions to or omissions from this list requested by the client should be made at this stage before the firms are approached.

When approval of the list has been received from your client, it is important that each firm is invited to submit a tender under similar conditions. It is essential, therefore, that:

1 They know the name of the client on whose behalf you are inviting tenders, and the address of the site.
2 That they agree to enter into direct contract with the client if there is a design element in their service, or for nomination in relationship to the type of general contract to be adopted.
3 They are provided with all necessary information on drawings.
4 The works to be done are clearly defined and accurately described.
5 They are to take into account the appropriate contract discounts in their estimate.
6 They are made aware of access to the site and the probable date on which works will be required to start on the site which will be subject to confirmation when the main contractor is appointed.
7 Where possible, they are given the opportunity to, and should, visit the site.
8 They know that it is a sub-contract to a main contract and agree to the contract terms under which the main works are to be carried out and that, if successful, the official order will ultimately be placed by the general contractor.
9 They have a time and date by which the tenders are to be returned to the architect and a specified period of validity.

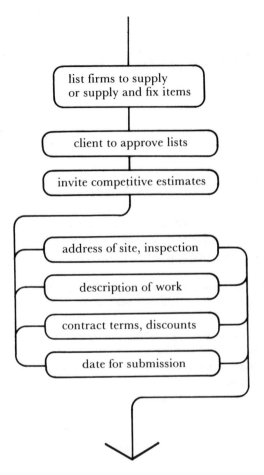

In reply they should be asked to give:
1 At least three copies of their quotation.
2 Their delivery date from the time of order.
3 Anticipated time required for the works on the site. } where fixing on
4 A description of builder's works required and attendance.} site

Copies of all documents as sent out to each firm should be kept in the office. As the procedure for inviting tenders should follow the pattern required of the building contract to be adopted, it is advisable to use the associated forms.

36

Sub-contractor nomination

Acknowledge receipt of all tenders immediately. If, during the period of tendering, there is a request for extension of time it must, if granted, be given to all the firms tendering for that part of the work.

When all tenders are received they should each be checked either by yourself or by the quantity surveyor against the original set of drawings in respect of areas or numbers of items, to ensure that each complies with the general terms of the invitation to tender. They should then be checked arithmetically and finally analysed one against the other under headings which include:

1 Total figure.
2 Price per unit of measurement (linear, area or itemised).
3 Percentage discount and compliance with terms of contract.
4 Delivery.
5 Length of time required on the site.
6 Attendance required and builder's work involved.
7 Conditions of tender if not in accordance with contract terms given and whether the firm is prepared to amend these to comply.
8 Closing date for acceptance of tenders. The QS will probably wish to report on these.

Copies of the sub-contract tender documents should be sent to the client with recommendations and a request for instructions to nominate the successful firms. Successful firms should be informed that, subject to acceptance, they will receive the official order for the work through the general contractor when he is appointed. The unsuccessful firms should be informed as soon as the decisions are made.

It is important that you do not officially place the order for the work. The general contractor places the order, enters into sub-contract, and instructs the sub-contractor direct.

Where drawings or details are to be prepared by a sub-contractor, this early selection, pending sub-contract arrangements by the general contractor, provides the opportunity for discussion and for the drawings to be prepared and checked as part of the general drawings' programme before the main contract is placed. Items related to the work, including such things as the amount of agreed tolerance, can then also be settled.

Samples of all materials being used should be kept in the office, for comparison with the work on the site, throughout the course of the contract.

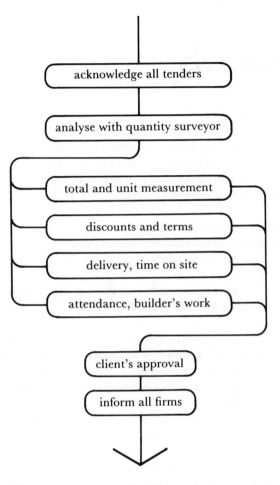

37
Cost records

During the course of the contract, prices invited will become available for all the sub-contract work on the building. Information concerning the lowest on each sub-contract should be abstracted and itemized for future reference in the office for estimating purposes on other contracts.

Information abstracted should include:
1 The price per unit measurement or cost per item.
2 Area, number of items, or quantity.
3 Location of contract.
4 Name, address and telephone number of company (and representative).
5 The date on which the estimate was obtained.

These should be kept up to date by replacing existing information with new estimates as they come into the office on any contract. It should work as a comprehensive guide to most aspects of construction and should include materials, components, mechanical services, specialist equipment or installations of any kind, furnishing or internal finishes.

This system should work in conjunction with a similar analysis of items which have been selected for the schedules. In an office where the collection of this data is being made on a number of contracts simultaneously by a number of assistants, it is sensible to abstract the illustrations from trade catalogues of those items which are regularly selected and form a reference system of them. Each illustration should be completed with its manufacturer, address, representative, telephone number, current price (dated), and reference number. As items are neglected, superseded or otherwise become out of date, the illustrations and information should be replaced. This particularly applies to sanitary fittings, electrical items, ironmongery and other supply items.

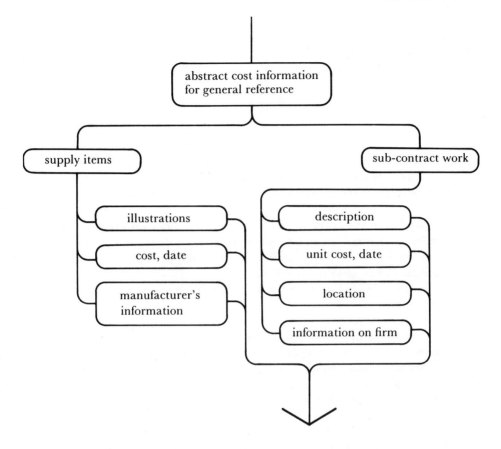

38

Insurances

The articles of agreement forming part of the contract between the client and contractor will state the types of insurance which each is obliged to undertake. These, however, are only the minimum required to comply with the conditions of the contract, and the client should at the same time be informed of any other risk which may exist and on which he should consult his insurance advisers. Depending upon whether the works are to be carried out in an existing building or are new premises, information which your client is likely to require includes:

(a) Dates on which the works are likely to start and finish.
(b) Estimated costs of works and fees.
(c) Classification of building for fire and loading.
(d) Security devices—locks, window catches.
(e) Day and night security arrangements.
(f) Any arrangements made with adjoining owners.
(g) 'Incidentals'—insurance against risks which would automatically become the liability of the employer where it is proved that the contractor has taken every reasonable precaution.
(h) Any other risks peculiar to the type or work.

For his own information you should also inform your client of any:
(a) Hoardings, pavement screens, projecting gantries or equipment.
(b) Overtime in premises occupied by other tenants.

Additional copies of the drawings should be sent for your client to deposit with the insurance company if required.

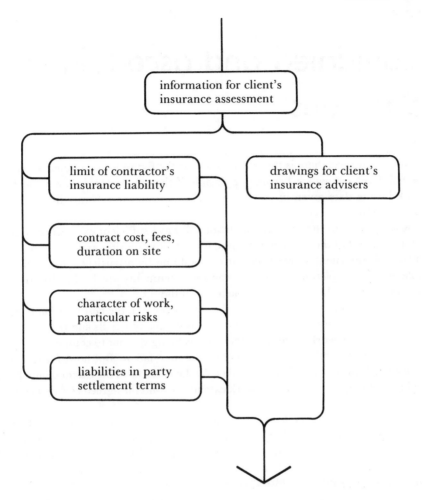

39

Liquidated and ascertained damages

In most contracts there is the option to insert the figure for liquidated and ascertained damages, which become applicable if the contractor does not finish the work by the date given in the document, or within the contract time properly extended by the architect.

Most people in the consultancy team will have sufficient experience to make an assessment of the construction time for the work on site, and taking into consideration the client's own need for the building by a particular date, they are able to set a completion date for the contract documents which will allow the contractor a reasonable time to complete the building.

The argument against this is that the contractor is in the best position to assess the construction period in relationship to his company's skills and resources, and approach to the work. Indeed, if the work is being put out to competitive tender one of the competitive elements may be the time factor. But however time is to be assessed, the decision has to be taken by the client as to the extent of any financial loss he may incur if the site work extends beyond the agreed contract completion date.

It can be said that the least loss would be interest on capital, for which a formula based upon the likely total contract sum and the assessed contract period related to the bank rate can give some indication, but the loss, if any, largely depends entirely on the building itself. Failure to construct an hotel on time would incur a considerable loss, just as continuity of working and transfer of staff from existing office premises to a new office building requires a pre-planned operation that would seriously be disrupted if delayed, and particularly so if lease termination arrangements were involved and short term alternative accommodation had to be found. The assessment of liquidated and ascertained damages must however be seen to be totally realistic and in no way a penalty. The insertion of a liquidated and ascertained damages sum in a contract acknowledges it to be an agreed loss, and entitles deduction from endorsed certificates issued by the architect in favour of the contractor, when justified by genuine failure to finish on time.

Two further points are worth noting; first, that any assessment of the construction operation should also take into account the follow-up work of cleaning, carpeting and furnishing, which can easily be under-estimated, between completion of the building and occupation. This does not affect the contractor, but will need to be brought into a client's own time assessments. Second, and most important, is that the contract period on site can only be established if the date of commencement is set by the insertion of a date for possession in the contract.

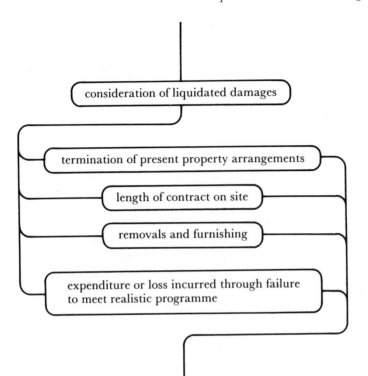

40

Clerk of works' appointment

The architect's terms of appointment assume periodic inspection of the work on site. Where your client requires, or where you recommend constant inspection, other than where the work calls for the additional services of a site architect, it should be pointed out that a clerk of works should be employed as the client's personal representative on the site. He is employed directly by the client and paid by him and, when he is taken on, the terms of his employment (which should be confirmed by your client) should state his working hours, holidays, and travelling time, and expenses if he lives in another part of the country. It is desirable, if the client wishes to interview applicants, that you are present. You may be asked to make recommendations on how to find and employ a clerk of works. This is usually done by advertising in the local press or technical journals, or approaching the Clerk of Works' Institute. Give advice on this early enough to allow time for advertising, interviews, appointment and instruction before the general contractor moves on to the site.

Remember that there is a distinction between the act of inspection, which can be delegated to the clerk of works, and the architect's overriding responsibility, which cannot be delegated. The clerk of works' responsibility is to make himself aware of all aspects of the work on site and to keep the architect informed.

The clerk of works will act in direct liaison with the architect and client and ideally, when appointed, should spend enough time in the architect's office with the person who will be responsible for the day-to-day running of the contract, to become familiar with all information including drawings, estimates, bills of quantities, etc., as well as the principles behind the design, detailing and construction system.

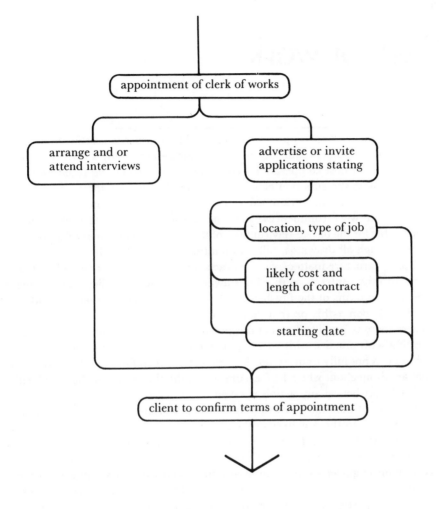

41
Clerk of works

When the clerk of works is appointed you should introduce yourself with a letter enumerating the points requiring special attention—essentially a briefing letter. To ensure the utmost co-operation and avoid misunderstanding resulting from a failure to state the situation clearly, the letter should state that:

1 It is desirable that the clerk of works spends a period of time in the architect's office before work commences, when he can meet the architect who will be responsible for the day-to-day running of the contract. This time will allow him to go through all drawings, bills of quantities, any local authority conditions and party structure matters, sub-contracts, any specialist work and other items related to the contract, so that he is aware of the design policy and its interpretation in terms of the finished building. Arrangements should be made to do this as soon as his present employment permits.

2 Where there is any likelihood of misinterpretation of detail due to its not conforming with practice with which he is familiar, it may be that the principle behind it is not fully understood. It is important, therefore, that he recognizes that anything about which he feels uneasy on the site should be discussed with the architect before any action is taken.

3 It is essential that the clerk of works, when working on the site, refers all discrepancies to the architect's office for decision.

4 It is important that a day-to-day diary is kept on the site in order that any representative from the architect's office, the quantity surveyor's office, or the consultant engineer's office can at any time follow the complete case history of the job. Entries should include details of hidden work, portions of work carried out by particular trades, any queries which have arisen, state of weather, number of men on the job, instructions given by anyone visiting the site with authority to do so, visitors to the site and the clerk of works' own activities. Copies of these entries should be sent to the architect and to the quantity surveyor weekly.

He should also be given a complete set of drawings and, in due course, a copy of the bills of quantities and articles of agreement under which the works are to be carried out, with the positive instruction that all site domestic matters must be settled in accordance with these.

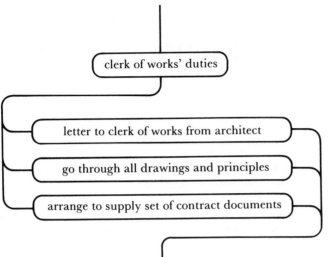

clerk of works' duties

letter to clerk of works from architect

go through all drawings and principles

arrange to supply set of contract documents

42

Compiling tender list

Main contractors to be listed for competitive tendering should be selected with extreme care and generally in accordance with the following principles:

1 Careful investigation is to be made to ensure that the firms listed are of equal capability, size and reputation.
2 Their selection by the client or you must be made without prejudice.
3 The firms and their previous works should preferably be known to you, or, alternatively, recommendation should be sought only of a person whose knowledge of the firm is sound.
4 Where their work is unknown, the firms should be asked to submit a list of contracts carried out with the names and addresses of three of the architects or clients from whom references can be obtained. The buildings should be inspected and where necessary an appointment made to visit the contractors' offices and yards.
5 When taking up references it is advisable to ask specifically for answers on such matters as contractors' office/site liaison, co-operation with sub-contractors, quality of workmanship in all trades, time, costs and extras.
6 The client must be fully informed of the system of selection and he must approve the list of those contractors recommended by you.
7 The client must be given the opportunity to add to the list, but only in accordance with the principles on which the others were selected.
8 The client should be warned not to contact or allow any staff communication with any of the selected firms before or while tendering is in progress.
9 The client must be informed that, although he is under no obligation to accept the lowest or any tender submitted, the system is devised to produce the most fair and well-balanced results on an equal basis to both client and contractor, and there would have to be a very good reason if the lowest tender were not to be adopted.

When the list is agreed between client and architect, the contractors should each be asked in good time whether they are prepared to submit competitive tenders.

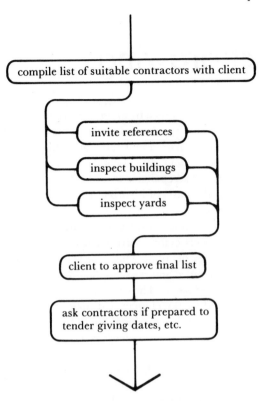

The invitation to tender may take a standard form, but in any case the contractors being invited should be given the following information:

Job ....

Building owner ....

Quantity surveyor ....

Consultants with supervisory duties ....

Location of site ....

General description of works ....

Form of contract ....

Proposed date for possession ....

Period for completion of works ....

Date for despatch of all tender documents ....

Date for submission of tender ....

It has been said that this is probably the most important 'five minutes' in any contract. It is certainly the time when an error of judgment can permit the inclusion on the list of an unsuitable firm whose success can cause serious problems for as long as the job is in progress and, in many cases, for some time after the building is occupied. Any doubts which arise at this time, however slight, must be cleared or the name crossed off the list.

43

Contract drawings

Drawings coming into your own office from any source must be checked carefully against your own drawings, to ensure that both read together in answering all queries that could possibly arise about the work when these drawings reach a building site. This must be done quickly, but accurately, and the sender informed immediately of any discrepancies in order to prevent his doing further work in his own office on the basis of incorrect dimensions, details or notation. When the correction affects your own drawings, copies of your amended drawing should be issued at the same time. Discrepancies should, however, be carefully investigated in all their aspects before correction, to avoid making a superficial amendment affecting complex detailing which cannot be adjusted on other drawings. A drawing which is amended and reissued should have its amendments clearly noted and be renumbered and dated. The drawing must also be issued to everyone whose work will be affected by the change. Estimates which are affected by the amendments should be revised. Instructions should be issued where sub-contract or other drawings need to be revised to follow the amendment and checked again after revision.

By this time all the drawings which have been prepared in your own office, or by consultants or sub-contractors, should form a comprehensive and complementary set of documents. At this point they can be seen as the final contract drawings. Before issuing these to the quantity surveyor for preparation of his bills of quantities, as well as going through construction, damp-proofing and weatherings throughout, a general check through all other information should be made as follows:

1 Read through all files from the beginning to see that instructions given from time to time have been incorporated on drawings or, alternatively, will be written into the bills of quantities. Check health and safety file items.

2 See that all consents have been received and that all terms of consents have been complied with.

3 Check against spelling errors, muddled dimensions or notation, or discrepancies between one drawing and another or on the schedules.

4 Ensure that all reference numbers for sub-contract items or British Standards are correct at the date of issue.

Finally, and before regarding the drawings as complete:

(a) Go through each item as it is to be used by the occupants on completion and correct all inconsistencies (e.g. a tap position too low to get a bucket into a cleaner's sink, or the centre line of a skirting socket outlet shown at a dimension from finished floor level where the height of the skirting conflicts).

(b) Go through the drawings as a site agent would set out the job, construct the work or order material, to see if all the information is adequate.

(c) Go through the drawings as a quantity surveyor would check a claim against a loosely specified section of work.

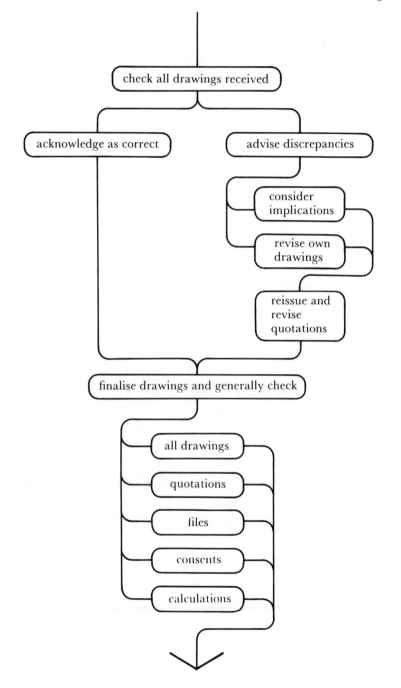

44

Quantity surveyor brief

Information required by the quantity surveyor for the preparation of his bills of quantities but not necessarily shown on the drawings will include:

1 Copies of the consents where clauses need to be incorporated in the bills and advice on appropriate fees or costs.
2 Copy of the building owner's or agents' specification requirements or tenancy conditions.
3 Details of party settlements or conditions of access to adjoining properties.
4 Survey of existing site (should include levels and details of existing drainage) or buildings with photographs.
5 Details of access to the site or any site restrictions (not forgetting arrangements for inspection by the contractor when tendering).
6 All details of the contract terms of agreement, including information on the form of contract to be used and, after discussion with your client, all the information on those clauses which make specific arrangements, such as insurance, arbitration and appendix items.
7 Facilities required if a clerk of works is to be employed on the site.
8 Copies of all agreed sub-contract or suppliers' estimates.

Discuss with your client the possible need to include provisional sums to cover mock-up work or progress and maintenance photography in the bills as part of the contract. Include an allowance in the bills of quantities for all the tests you will require on materials during the course of the work, and give details of the types of tests and methods of carrying them out. Remember that mock-ups are the nearest to prototypes that the building industry can get, and the maximum advantage should be taken of their benefits, consistent with the type of job.

The contractor will be pricing the work primarily on the basis of the information given to him in the bills. It is essential, therefore, that everything he needs to know for the complete operation is included in the information given by you to the quantity surveyor, at this stage, for the preparation of full bills of quantities.

Check the final arrangements for the length of time to be devoted to:

1 Analysis and measurement of all drawings and information and preparation of bills by the quantity surveyor.
2 Printing of bills.
3 Tendering.
4 Contract negotiations and approval by client.
5 Placing the contract and starting work on site.

Send copies of all the completed drawings and information to your client for final comment and records immediately before issuing them to the quantity

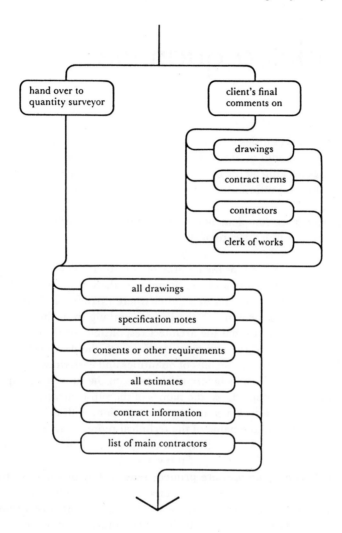

surveyor.

Inform the quantity surveyor at this stage how many copies of the bills of quantities will be required, remembering the client and his agents, the contractor and the clerk of works.

From the moment the quantity surveyor is given this contract information, copies of all letters, instructions and drawings issued from your office, and any revised quotations or other information in respect of the contract, should be sent to the quantity surveyor's office until the termination of the contract. This enables him to follow the course of the work and to abstract all relevant information as it affects measurement of the works in progress on the site, or anything else which will affect the final account.

45

Completed quantities

When the bills of quantities have been completed in draft form, and before they are printed, you should go through the documents with the quantity surveyor, carefully cross-checking all the drawings and transferring to your own drawings, in the form of notes, information which amplifies that already on the drawings. These, related to their appropriate sections of construction, ensure that the two sets of documents are complementary and that the man working from the drawing on the site is as much aware of specific bills of quantities notation as the site agent.

Whilst it is appreciated that the contractor is responsible for conveying all information to sub-contractors and site operatives, there is a case for duplicating information from one document to another where there is any likelihood of full information not being available to the person working from the drawing. This general check also ensures that the architect responsible for the day-to-day running of the contract, and the assistants dealing with the drawings in the office, see the relationship between the bills of quantities and each drawing and become fully acquainted with the bills before work starts on the site. Where appropriate to the contract to be adopted, list the names of the sub-contractors or suppliers, as acceptable and open to the contractor for selection, with their addresses and telephone numbers and the name of the technical representative with whom the work has been discussed. This gives the contractor, when nominated, the appropriate contacts for all sections of the work.

When the bills of quantities are printed, send a copy or copies to the client, as pre-arranged, for his information and records. When he has approved them, and depending upon arrangements made in your preliminary discussions, either instruct the quantity surveyor to issue them to contractors for tenders or prepare the appropriate documents for issuing from your own office.

It should be noted that this is the last point at which delay costs relatively little. Once the contract is placed all changes and delays cost money.

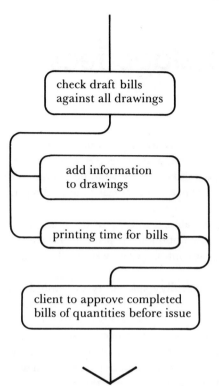

46

Contract stage fees

The completion of all information to a stage sufficiently advanced to place the contract is customarily a major fee stage. It may also be a point at which the staged payments become linked to the building operation on the site. Assuming that fees are being charged in a conventional manner as a percentage of the building cost, the fee will be based upon the latest estimated cost of the building in accordance with the originally agreed scale, plus the reimbursable expenses incurred from the date of the presentation of the previous fee statement, if presenting the account before placing the contract. Otherwise it will be based on the figure entered in the contract.

The account should be fully explanatory in listing in some detail the stages through which the work has passed up to the presentation of the account, and should also list the headings under which reimbursable expenses are being claimed; the appropriate tax, and the architect's tax registration number.

Consultants will generally have made their own arrangements with the client for direct staged payments in accordance with their own independent institutional recommendations. Where they have not, this is a convenient point at which to ensure that all fees and expenses due to the consultants up to this stage are submitted and forwarded to the client for clearance.

Where it is not otherwise a regular practice procedure in the office, this is also a good time to undertake cost checks of architectural, technical staff, and overhead costs against the fee accounts submitted.

From this point onwards, and to ensure that professional fees are charged up to the value of work on site, but not in excess of the work still to be done, the remainder of the fee to the end of the job can be related to valuations and certificates issued as interim payments for the contractor. This is generally convenient both to the architect and the client, and becomes a matter of issuing a fee statement to the client concurrently with certificates to the contractor based upon the value of the work.

Remember to note on all fee statements that the final fee will be adjusted to relate to the final account.

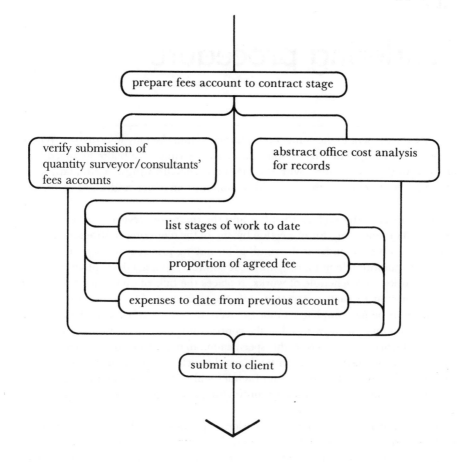

47
Tendering procedure

The documents sent to the competing contractors must be fully informative. Where the contract comprises bills of quantities and drawings, the blank itemized bills are sent to the contractors, with the main advisory drawings. A standard form of tender is attached to the bill, with a standard envelope addressed to the architect's office. A full set of contract drawings and documentation should be available in both the architect's office and the quantity surveyor's office during the period of tendering, for inspection by any of the tendering contractors. A contractor's lump sum tender is the result of his having priced every item in the bill.

Where quantities do not form part of the contract, a totally descriptive specification of works, or a schedule of works, replaces the bills of quantities and is sent out for pricing to each contractor with the drawings. The importance of the specification being complete cannot be overstressed, as it is on the basis of the specification and the drawings that the contractor builds up his lump sum tender price, and work not covered by this specification may be claimed to be a justifiable extra on the contract. A form of tender and envelope will be included as in the case with quantities, and the form of tender will in both cases be the single item which is returned from competing contractors, giving the lump sum cost for the work.

Standard forms are available for tendering purposes, and generally their contents include the name of the job, description of work and the name of the employer. On the form the contractors are required to state that they have read the conditions of contract and bills of quantities, that they have examined the drawings and offer to execute and complete works in accordance with the contract for the total sum, which they then insert. They give a construction period of the number of weeks from the date of possession of the site, and undertake in the event of acceptance of the tender to execute with the client the formal contract embodying the conditions and terms contained in the offer. The tender form requires them to state the period for which their tender will remain open for consideration. This is generally 28 days from the date of submission. The tender is signed and witnessed ready to take its place as a contract document if the tender is successful.

The form and documents where comprising drawings and specification are generally sent out to contractors by the architect, but frequently by the quantity surveyor where bills of quantities have been prepared. In both cases the return envelope is addressed to the architect.

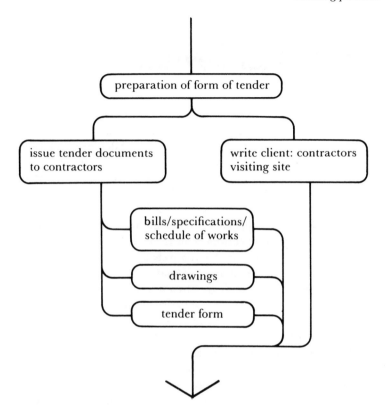

The health and safety plan must be sent to or be available for inspection by competing contractors in order that they may assess needs for their own contract arrangements.

48

Pre-contract review

Everyone concerned with a contract which is out to tender feels slightly apprehensive about the results. In competitive tendering so many external factors can affect the way in which contractors cost their work. Early estimates received from sub-contract tenders and the cost reviews which have been prepared at intervals by the quantity surveyor should give enough information for reasonable prediction, but factors like regional slackness in the building industry can suddenly produce much more competitive costing than is good for the benefit of the client, or indeed the successful contractor. Alternatively a job requiring a quality of finish only available from particular contractors may have suggested the invitation of tenders from a group of firms who are already very busy and unable to take on more work. In some cases a contractor will price himself out with too high a tender in order to remain on tendering lists, rather than withdrawing from the list and possibly not being asked again.

It is helpful before the tenders are received to prepare with the quantity surveyor a review which brings everything up to date as nearly as it is possible to predict; to schedule the sub-contract and supply estimates received, which gives the opportunity to see the relationship between the measured and other work in the contract and to list the sums set aside for mock-ups, tests, the contingency sum and other supporting items. Changes made for any reason during design development should also be noted and the cost element shown, and if not already included in interim cost reviews, any inflationary changes which have already taken place or are likely to affect the price during the construction period of the work.

Finally, consideration should be given to the state of tendering on other work in the architect's or consultants' offices to see whether anything there may reflect on the results of tenders being prepared.

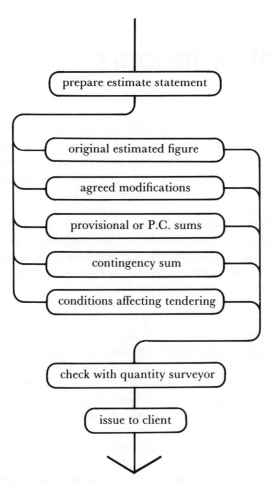

49

Receipt of tenders

While tenders are usually addressed to the architect, the client, the quantity surveyor and contractors are entitled, though rarely take up the option, to be present when competitive tenders are opened. They must be opened at the time noted in the tender form and those arriving late must be excluded. It is never possible to make an immediate decision, however, as details can only be discussed after the quantity surveyor's report following examination of the priced bills related to the lowest tender. All tenders should be acknowledged immediately. The contractor who has submitted the lowest tender should be asked to send in his priced bills of quantities to the quantity surveyor for examination. The contractor submitting the second lowest tender should be asked to hold his tender open until the lowest has been verified. As soon as the lowest bill has been received, the quantity surveyor should prepare a report which covers an arithmetical check of the lowest and comments upon any conditions of tender which may have been inserted by contractors. Forward this to the client with your recommendations and advice on which tender to accept. Ask for the client's instructions to make the appointment on his behalf and prepare the contract documents in accordance with the tender submitted. Where an error in pricing is discovered in the lowest tender, the contractor should be informed. He has the option of withdrawing his tender, in which case the next lowest is examined; or he can stand by his tender or correct genuine errors. If his tender is not then lowest, the next should be examined. It is not good policy either for him to stand by a serious error due to the possible repercussions throughout the contract, or for you to recommend its acceptance to the client; but, where the contractor wishes to stand by an error of no great significance, the contract price must remain as submitted. Corrections must, however, be made to the documents by the quantity surveyor as necessary, solely for use in pricing variations to the contract. When the contractor has been appointed, the other contractors should immediately be informed. Give a list of the prices received in descending order but without names so that they are able to see how their price compares with others.

The same principles apply to tenders submitted on the basis of priced documents where there are no bills of quantities.

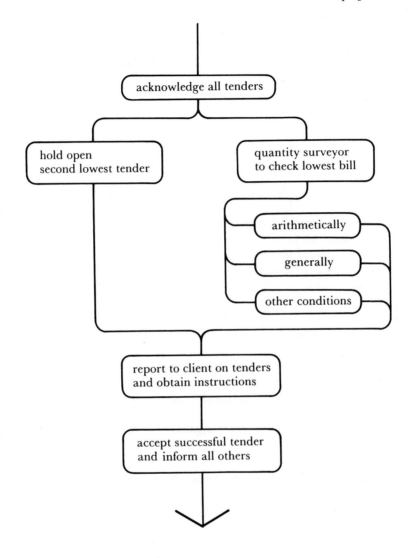

50

Preparation of contract documents

Prepare the contract documents as soon as the client has given approval to the tendering report. Taking the two principal forms of lump sum contract as examples, the contract documents will comprise:
1 Where no quantities have been prepared:
   (a) The form of tender.
   (b) The drawings on which the contractor tendered.
   (c) The specification or schedule of works which has been priced by the contractor in tendering.
   (d) The chosen Articles of Agreement for use without quantities.
2 Where quantities have been prepared:
   (a) The form of tender.
   (b) The principal drawings from which quantities were prepared.
   (c) The priced bills of quantities.
   (d) The chosen Articles of Agreement for use with quantities.

The documents should be prepared in duplicate so that the contractor will have a true copy of the originals.

The Articles of Agreement being adopted must be completed and all amendments signed by each party in accordance with the conditions printed in the documents on which the contractor tendered. Where the Articles are to be executed under hand by written signature no stamp is necessary. If as a deed, the original must be impressed by the Inland Revenue within thirty days of the contract. The execution of a contract is when it is completed by the second party.

While it is usually the case that a limited company must execute a contract as a deed, this is not invariable, as certain company articles allow a contract up to a fixed figure to be executed by hand. Where both parties are limited companies and one wishes to execute the contract by hand, check that the other company has authority to do so before agreeing. Drawings and bills of quantities or other priced document comprising contract documents should all be marked as the contract documents referred to in the Articles of Agreement. they should be signed by each party to the contract and dated.

Where a clerk of works is employed by the client, he should be provided with a copy of the completed but unstamped Articles of Agreement under which the work is to be carried out, for information throughout the contract.

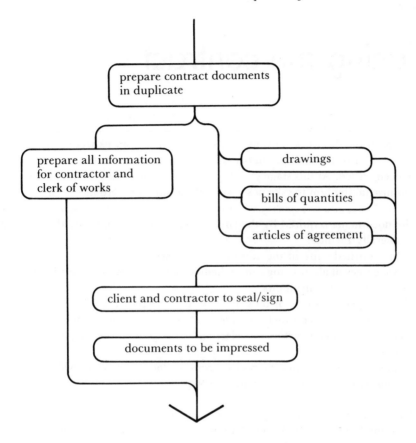

51
Placing the contract

To programme the work sensibly and set the contract on its feet efficiently, the contractors must have all the information as soon as the contract arrangements have been settled. At this stage you should write to the contractor on your client's behalf instructing him to take possession of the site in accordance with the terms of the contract, and to proceed with the work. You should at the same time issue all the documents required by the specific terms of agreement used, but which will generally include:

(a) One certified copy of the contract document.
(b) Two copies of all drawings and schedules for the work, including those from engineers and consultants.
(c) Two unpriced copies of bills of quantities/specification/schedule of works.
(d) The appropriate contract forms for sub-contractor nomination/the listed as approved sub-contractors for selection by the general contractor as domestic sub-contractors.
(e) Copies of consents and the notices from the local authorities which are to be submitted throughout the course of work.

The letter of instruction should give general information on the contract including the name and telephone number of the architect in the office who will be primarily concerned with general enquiries, site inspection and the day-to-day running of the contract. Give the name of the clerk of works, and the names of local authority officials with whom you have been in contact in respect of consents etc.

Draw the contractor's attention to the terms of any party settlements which have been made with adjoining owners. Ask for a draft programme of works to be prepared as soon as all the information has been assimilated including sub-contract work so that detailed programming can be developed.

Make it a specific instruction that every query, however small, should be referred to the clerk of works who has instructions to contact the architect in all cases, or alternatively, where no clerk of works, to refer all queries directly to the architect's office. This instruction is essential because, although it is noted in the bills of quantities, a new site agent or clerk of works is often reluctant to refer queries to the architect in case the answer is obvious.

Ask for insurance premium receipts to be submitted for inspection in accordance with contract terms.

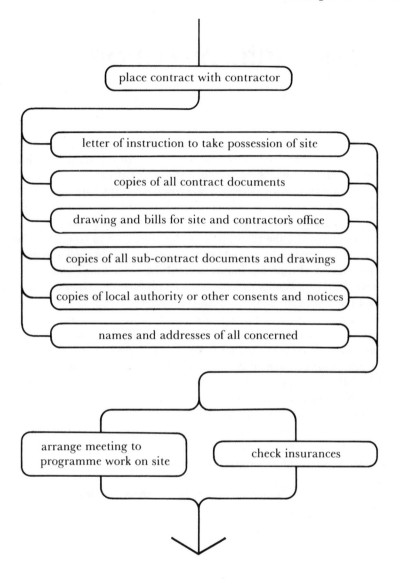

place contract with contractor

letter of instruction to take possession of site

copies of all contract documents

drawing and bills for site and contractor's office

copies of all sub-contract documents and drawings

copies of local authority or other consents and notices

names and addresses of all concerned

arrange meeting to programme work on site

check insurances

52

Contract interpretation

As soon as the contract arrangements have been completed, it is important that the client is informed by letter of the change of role for the architect. This is the point at which the architect becomes the arbitrator between the contractor and client in assessing and taking decisions according to the interpretation of the contract throughout the rest of the work. In order to fulfil this role he may possibly at times be acting against the general interests of the client and, although still technically employed by the client, he is under obligation to administer the contract impartially according to its true intent. This particularly applies to such situations as extensions of time for causes beyond the contractor's control.

You have the responsibility to settle contract problems by objectively applying the terms under which the Articles of Agreement were accepted and it is essential that your client is forewarned of this obligation as he is, in many cases, rather less willing than the contractor to accept a decision against him.

It is not generally appreciated by architects, however, that just as limitation of their skills requires them to draw the client's attention to the need for consultants for different aspects of the work—so it is incumbent upon them to suggest reference to legal advisers where a clause comes under serious questioning and beyond daily administrative knowledge.

At this stage the architect or quantity surveyor should advise the client of the approximate amounts which are likely to be included in certificates, and to remind him of the likely dates of presentation of certificates so that he may make banking arrangements accordingly.

Inform the client that under no circumstances should he instruct the contractor or any of his men direct.

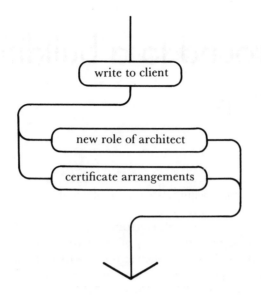

53
Background to a building operation

A building operation may begin relatively simply, with a client and an architect, but it rapidly collects over a few months the services of cost, structural and services consultants, and before long also recruits a large number of companies, many of whom become advisers on the supply of specialist services, materials or components. These firms, multiplied as often as is necessary to achieve the appropriate level of competition, represent a very large team even before the architect has placed the contract. With the appointment of the general contractor's organization, a project of even modest proportions will involve hundreds of people, so recognition of the way in which delayed action or imprecision can create widespread problems is an important starting point.

No architect likes to admit it, but regrettably it has to be acknowledged that the creative part of the work should be over when the job starts on the site. The work of management and inspection is to ensure the best results within the conditions embodied in the documents which describe the buildings and the contract terms within which it is carried out.

Once the contract is signed there is a significant change. The contractor, who may already have been an important contributor to consultants' meetings, will now with his supporting sub-contract companies, become the constructor. The architect, engineer, services consultant and quantity surveyor in one way or another become inspectors. While the essence of a well-conducted construction operation must remain collaboration, the overlap of these two distinct areas of responsibility must be discouraged; the contractor may become only too willing to let the architect sort out (and acquire responsibility for) the sub-contractor's problems, while the architect may be perfectly happy to let the contractor resolve (and relieve the architect of his responsibility for) a difficult drain detail.

The terms of agreement and contract documents largely predetermine the basic rules for the building operation, and in turn the individual responsibilities of the participants and the degree of authority that goes with those responsibilities.

From the point when the contract is signed, the architect becomes the contact point for the client and consultant team, and is obliged to stop dealing directly with the sub-contractors and suppliers with whom he has been working up to the date of the preparation of the bills of quantities. The general contractor now takes over and co-ordinates the work of sub-contractors and suppliers, and becomes the complementary contact point for the whole of the construction side of the operation.

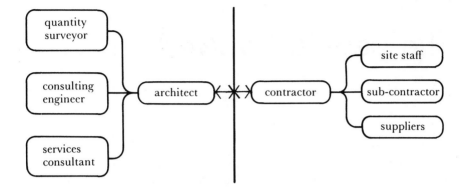

54
The people involved

The client must be regarded as a member of the design group. Up to the contract stage he has worked closely with the architect and consultants. The contract documents, drawings and bills of quantities and supporting documents describe the building he wants. He has undertaken to pay a specific sum for it. But his functions after the contract is signed are limited. He must allow the architect the appropriate authority to act as his agent. He must pay within the time specified in the contract those sums which are certified by the architect as due to the contractor. Having authorized the architect to act on his behalf, he should issue instructions only through the architect and must be available to the architect for any decisions in order that proper control of the job and therefore the price can be maintained on his behalf.

The architect continues to co-ordinate the job as a whole, and the work of the other consultants; to this he adds the work of inspecting the building construction as the job proceeds on site and instructing as necessary. In doing this he must recognize that the site and the work on it are the total responsibility of the contractor, from the date of possession until the building is handed over. The architect's duties on site are to ensure that the contractor is doing his utmost to comply with the instructions given to him in drawings, bills and other contract documents, and that the quality of workmanship and materials does not fall below the minimum standard specified.

He is not entitled to accept less than is described in the contract. Neither can he claim more from the contractor than has been drawn, specified or is to be paid for. He releases certificates of payment on account for work properly executed to the contractor, on the bases of advisory valuations made by the quantity surveyor which will also include payments to sub-contractors, and where confirmed as agreed, for work under the direction of other consultants.

The quantity surveyor's responsibilities after the contract is placed are in the accurate control of measurement and valuation of work as it proceeds on the site. It is on the basis of these valuations that the architect issues his interim certificates of payment to the contractor at the intervals prearranged in the contract documents. The quantity surveyor is also responsible for the preparation of the final account.

The engineer, from his own specialist knowledge, must ensure that the work carried out complies fully with his intentions. He will issue instructions concerning his own work through the architect's office in accordance with the contract. He also works with the quantity surveyor concerning the value of work or equipment within the area of his own consultancy. The inspection of his work may be carried out by regular site visits by a member of his office, or by a resident engineer from his office on the site full time. In either case a report/instruction from the site or a visit will follow a route back to the engineer's office and will be issued through architect's instructions. The engineer will work directly with local authorities concerning requests for structural calculations and will confirm the acceptability of test results, with reports to the architect, as the work proceeds. He will be required to confirm acceptance of his aspect of site work to the architect for certification.

The services consultant's work follows a similar pattern to that of the engineer with the same need for site reports, test confirmation, certificate confirmation and instruction through the architect's office.

The contract manager is responsible for the management of the work in the general contractor's company and is the direct counterpart of the architect responsible for the day to day running of the contract in the architect's office. It is through the contract manager that the architect works with the contracting company. It is from the contract manager that the site agent receives his instructions. From the day the contract is signed it is this man who has effective control of the entire building operation. In management terms he cannot be instructed beyond the scope of the contract documents.

He works in the contractor's main office and visits the site as he feels necessary for co-ordination and control of the site work. He keeps the site agent fully instructed and provided with everything necessary, and ensures that the work is being done in accordance with the agreed terms. Depending on the size of firm he may be responsible for bringing together plant, materials and labour, arranging meetings, sub-contractors, programming, estimating and cost control.

The site agent has direct control of the whole site operation. He may have a number of trade foremen: a foreman bricklayer, a foreman joiner, etc. The teams in the various trades will take their orders for the detailed work from their trade foreman, who in the first instance has been instructed by the site agent.

Although the site agent is responsible for the work as a whole, he is primarily concerned with initiating each particular operation, co-ordinating it with the other trades and ensuring that it has a clear run and is supplied with the appropriate plant, labour and materials.

A sub-contractor on the site is in the same position as a separate trade, with his own foreman who has the same relationship with the main contractor's site agent as have the trade foremen.

The ideal site agent attempts to assess the work impartially and condemns what he regards to be bad work from his own men without waiting for the architect's view.

The site agent's immediate superior is the contracts manager through whom he conducts his entire business outside the site. His formal line of communication should be only with the contract manager in order that the records of the job are complete within the contractor's own organization.

The clerk of works' position differs from that of others in that he is not a member of either the design or construction group: he is officially appointed and paid by the client. He is an inspector for the client but acts under the direction of the architect. He cannot issue any instruction which the architect would not be empowered to issue, and when instructing on behalf of the architect such an instruction must be confirmed in writing by the architect.

The clerk of works is often but not necessarily a former site agent who has a sound working knowledge of the building industry and site works; he may have a fairly advanced knowledge of organization and administrative procedures. He has no subordinate; his authority lies in the careful balance of imparting knowledge to both architect and contractor: to the architect by maintaining accurate records, and to the contractor in anticipating the requirements of the programme, or a construction sequence, or in the interpretation of information. He keeps his eyes open and has no other ties. A clerk of works' functions are to inspect fully and to record adequately.

55

Contractor's programme

Job programming is a complicated piece of co-ordination of other people's efforts, which on large contracts is often based upon very sophisticated methods of analysis. The smallest job, however, demands that the general contractor undertakes close examination of the assessments of time and resources to be devoted to all sub trade operations with sub-contractors as a part of his own programme co-ordination. He will usually issue his draft programme for work in advance of meetings with all sub-contractors, to enable everyone to relate this to other work and plan their own sections of the work in their own office. Modifications or revisions can then be made around known conditions rather than firms' representatives agreeing for the sake of being helpful, periods which incur later delays which throw the whole contract off balance.

Each trade operation and sub-contract is normally shown in contract sequence, and the dates on which they start and finish on site. They therefore give a cross-section of the work on the site at any one time. A copy in the architect's office can then be related to clerk of works' or other site reports in checking progress, and ensures that subsequent site visits for inspection of work can be carefully related to particular sequences or stages in the contract. The programme is a forecast rather than a fact and must allow sufficient flexibility to ensure that departure from it does not spell disaster. It must be realistic in avoiding setting optimistic dates which will be difficult to meet. No building owner will be disappointed at having a building completed earlier than planned.

It must also be recognized that generally the only significant date in contract terms is the practical completion date, and if the programme drifts away without good reason during the progress of the work, the contractor is obliged to reconsider the sequence of work or any other aspect of the programme to ensure that the end date is met.

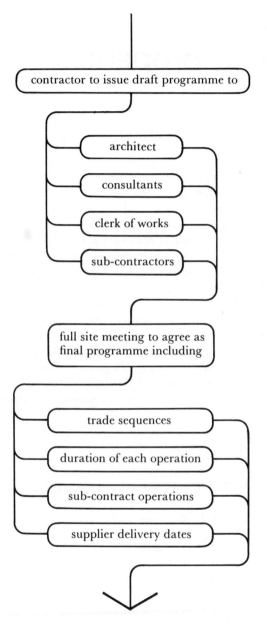

contractor to issue draft programme to

architect

consultants

clerk of works

sub-contractors

full site meeting to agree as final programme including

trade sequences

duration of each operation

sub-contract operations

supplier delivery dates

56
Adjoining properties

The site agent and the clerk of works should be carefully instructed on the terms of any agreement with adjoining owners concerning party structure work. Extreme care must be taken to ensure that there is no infringement of a boundary either in depth, plan area, height or sight line. The boundaries must be settled at the beginning and adhered to strictly throughout the contract.

An adjoining owner or neighbour has the right to expect that a contractor or anyone concerned with a building operation next door will have the courtesy to introduce themselves and not treat the adjoining property as if it were part of the site. They do not want materials hoisted over their building, leaned against their walls or stacked in front of their entrance. It is in the contractor's interest to take over the site in the most amicable way. The architect can help in this respect by writing letters informing adjoining owners when the contractor will be taking over the site. Most adjoining owners or neighbours will wish to know more about the building to be built beside them, so there is no harm in giving a description of it and enlisting their interest from the beginning, rather than allowing antagonism to develop with the increasing noise and disturbance of a nearby building operation. Offer to meet neighbours at any time during the course of the contract if there are any problems. Where party structures are affected, they will have been dealt with in advance of placing the contract, but even if they are not involved, it is as well to prepare a schedule of condition of the adjoining properties, if one has not already been prepared, to simplify any problems which might arise at a later date.

During the course of the works, the condition of adjoining properties should be checked against the schedule of condition to ensure that any necessary action can be taken. Dated 'telltales' should be applied to any cracks which exist, so that any evidence of movement is apparent. Movement of any kind should be investigated.

Any problems arising from works to a structure owned jointly by building owner and adjoining owner should at once become the subject of a combined inspection by the surveyors to both premises, and agreement reached (and confirmed) as to the way in which the matter is to be dealt with.

Arrangements will be made for a final inspection of the work carried out on party structures.

57

Site reports

An awareness of daily site conditions and progress is normally best maintained by adopting an arrangement in which reports are submitted to the architect's office weekly from the site, either by the clerk of works, where there is one, or alternatively by the contractor. This should take a standard form to give a clear and weekly comparable picture of the current stage of the work and anticipate anything on which the architect or contractor should be taking action. To do this, the report should include the following information:

(*a*) The main contractor's labour force on the site each day.

(*b*) The sub-contractors' labour force on the site each day.

(*c*) Materials delivered to the site and plant delivered or removed.

(*d*) Labour, plant or material shortages.

(*e*) Any delays or stoppages incurred and causes, with running totals.

(*f*) Daily state of weather including temperatures (from a thermometer not in direct sunlight).

(*g*) Visitors to the site and which day, with meetings noted.

(*h*) Date on which drawings or information received and notes of any information required.

(*i*) Notes on general progress related to programme.

In the absence of a clerk of works, it must be signed and dated by the person in charge of the works as a true record of the works for the week. These documents represent a job diary from the date when the contractor takes possession of the site until completion of the works. As such, it is the principal source of information for the maintenance of good progress, and, also, may subsequently be the basis on which claims are negotiated.

They are not to be regarded as dead documents for reference if anything goes wrong later, but for active consideration at the time in respect of the programme and to anticipate whatever action should be taken to avoid problems.

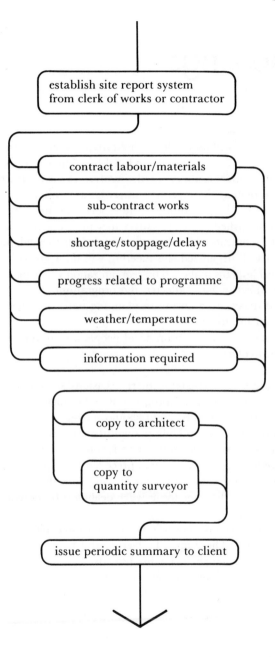

58

Site meetings

The general contractor will undoubtedly hold frequent site meetings in which he will be concerned with domestic issues related to sequence, resources and sub-contracts, but the architect is not generally involved in the contractor's organizational matters and regular site meetings otherwise are unnecessary when regular consultants' meetings, the programme, site reports and frequent site inspection visits have been established to ensure satisfactory progress in terms of the day-to-day running of the contract. There are certain periods throughout the contract, however, when a well organized site meeting will do a great deal to:

(a) give a renewed impetus to the job by reorganization where delays or difficulties are likely to affect or have affected the programme;

(b) help to avoid delay or confusion in planning particular operations with all concerned well in advance;

(c) solve site problems where a number of people are concerned or where cost or delay are involved.

Site meetings are best restricted to these occasions and should be called only when necessary to maintain good progress or settle outstanding problems.

A copy of the Articles of Agreement should be kept on site, together with a copy of the contract drawings and bills of quantities. Points in question may need to be considered in terms of the contract and while there is room for intelligent compromise, care must be taken to avoid precedent in bypassing contract conditions. Having ignored the contract on one or two points during an operation can make it difficult to apply the same terms when dealing with more important points in the final settlement.

Minutes should be taken with decisions recorded and copies of the minutes sent to everyone concerned. These must be factual and not include implications. A copy should be sent to the client for his records.

As, under the contract, the general contractor is responsible for the site and sub-contractors, he should arrange and run site meetings. The agenda will usually include the following:

1 Record of those attending.
2 Acceptance of previous minutes.
3 Items arising from previous minutes.
4 Progress related to programme.
5 Labour strength and materials queries.
6 Drawings received or due.
7 Sub-contracts.

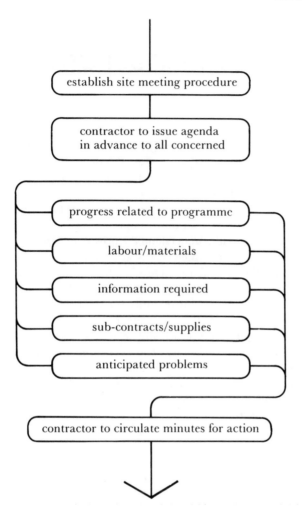

8 Financial review.
9 Any other business.
10 Date of next meeting—where known.

It is essential to include an 'action' column in the minutes so that there is no confusion as to who is responsible for dealing with each item.

59
Architect's instructions

The architect's instruction is the means by which the client, architect or consultants pass a contract instruction to the contractor. Whatever the origin, it is issued by the architect, with copies to the client and consultants. The instruction may be an amplification of information which is already in the contractor's hands, or it can affect both cost and time. Under the terms of contract adopted a specific procedure for instruction will be laid down, and although appropriate documents are published it is important to understand the principles. Any instructions which involve a variation in cost, or which clearly affect the length of time required for the contract, should aim to establish these at the time, while the facts are available and fresh in everyone's mind and in order that they are not left to be argued about at the end of the works. Ideally, the quantity surveyor should price the variation before the instruction is issued. This procedure ensures that as the work progresses an accurate cost account and time schedule can be maintained. It gives the opportunity of assessing in advance any action which may need to be taken in adjusting time or cost of operations. It is important, however, that variations in time should not be accounted in terms of cost of preliminaries until the final settlement of extended time at the point of practical completion. Subsequent settlements made from time to time should be noted in site meetings and copies distributed to your client, the quantity surveyor, the clerk of works and the contractor.

Where an extension of time is granted in accordance with the appropriate clauses of the Articles of Agreement, the attention of the contractor and client should be drawn to the need to extend their respective insurances. Where a client is tempted to save sums in the contract against increased spending elsewhere on works, he must be warned that the contractor tendered under the conditions printed in the bills and on works as noted on the drawings. The removal or omission of measured work does not relieve the client of a possible obligation to pay the percentage profit which the contractor could have expected on that section of the work. If he is likely to want to have the work done later, he would be best advised to leave it in the contract.

Similarly, when ordering work which automatically carries an extension of time, you must warn your client that it has been possible for a contractor to claim for being kept on site longer than he had anticipated.

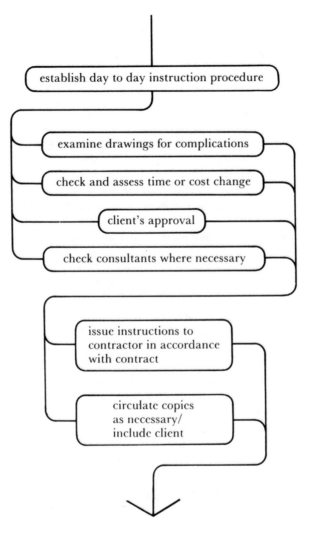

establish day to day instruction procedure

examine drawings for complications

check and assess time or cost change

client's approval

check consultants where necessary

issue instructions to
contractor in accordance
with contract

circulate copies
as necessary/
include client

60
Modifications

It is inevitable that during the course of the operation someone (who may well be the client) will want to make modifications, and these will be brought into effect in the form of a normal architect's instruction after proper investigation by the architect. The file copy of the instruction should be noted with the reason and the authority for modification in order that any extra cost or extension of time is fully recognized. It is the architect's duty to advise the client if the modification is likely to cause considerably more complication than is at first evident and to warn him of the possible results before issuing the instruction. A change, which seems to be only a simple operation to a client when looking at a small scale drawing, may have repercussions on the complete services system for the building, may be the critical point in the fire check arrangements or, though a simple building operation, may require the repositioning of the contractor's hoist system for the whole building. It is essential, therefore, that a thorough check of all drawings, schedules, bills of quantities and site works is made before advising your client. Against this it should be remembered regrettably that, from a client's point of view, it may be, though not always the case, considerably cheaper for him to change his mind during the course of a contract, than to have the work completed and a modification carried out independently. Even so, the client should be warned that an extension of time carries with it an extension of certain of the contractors' costs and that liquidated and ascertained damages, operating from the original date, will now operate from the extended date and may be rather harder to establish unless the modification is almost inevitable.

Where a modification is established which involves reissuing drawings, the drawing must attract specific attention to the modification. The author is aware of what he has done to revise a drawing, but unless advised, the recipient cannot easily identify revisions.

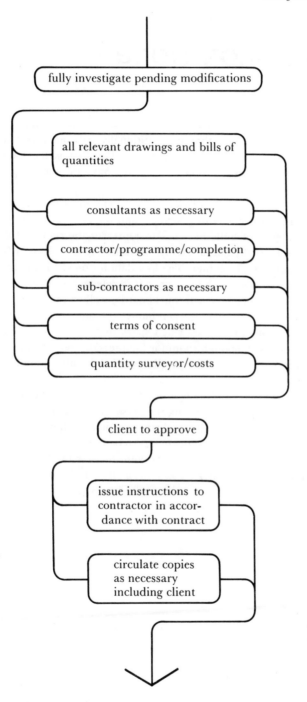

61

Foundation stone

There are three ceremonies that are traditionally associated with new buildings, and which most clients like to perpetuate. The first is the foundation stone ceremony, the second is the topping out ceremony, and the third is the opening ceremony.

The problem with the foundation stone ceremony is that the building needs to have progressed considerably further than the foundation stage before there is enough evidence of building work to represent the centre of the ceremony. However, it is generally not far enough advanced to be able to provide overhead cover in the case of bad weather. The foundation stone laying therefore becomes in effect a corner stone ceremony, since it is deferred to the stage when the site can be tidied up sufficiently with duckboards, walkways and temporary shelter to make it possible to conduct the ceremony with any appropriate sense of occasion. It usually calls for a platformed space to accommodate about six people around the stone with enough room for the press or photographers, and an area in which an invited audience of people associated with the building can watch the ceremony.

It is a client's event, and he will be responsible for invitations to guests and the principal participants, including the person who is to lay the stone. The contractor will need to know well in advance, as it will affect the operation of the site and require the special arrangements to be put in hand to accommodate the group of visitors. From a construction point of view the 'stone' is selected and specially prepared well in advance as it normally carries an inscription giving the date of the foundation stone laying and the name of the person laying it. A cavity is prepared in the stone itself, or alternatively is formed in association with the stonework construction, which can accommodate a container holding objects appropriate to the occasion and the building. The stone is dressed to contain a lid which can be firmly bedded on top of the container, sealing it in to the building.

The traditional form for the ceremony is that the building owner welcomes guests to the site and they are shown to the ceremony area. He then welcomes and conducts his principal guests to the platform prepared for the ceremony, introduces the ceremony itself and invites the principal guest to lay the foundation stone. The contractor has already bedded the stone in its true position, so the ceremony simply involves placing the container in the cavity and laying the prepared lid on to a mortar bed to seal the contents. Customarily the architect provides a silver trowel for this, inscribed to mark the occasion. The trowel is presented to the guest immediately after the introduction and invitation to lay the stone. When the lid has been placed, the contractor conventionally provides the inscribed maul with which to tap the stone home. This is normally presented by the site agent. The ceremony requires the stone layer to strike the stone lightly with the maul three times on each corner in an anti-clockwise direction, saying "in equity, justice, temperance and fortitude, I declare this stone well and truly laid" (one word at each corner). The ceremony is normally terminated by the building owner thanking the stone layer and the principal guests for attending. The stone is then given a protective cover to protect it during the remainder of the work.

62

Site progress photographs

However many site visits have been made during the progress of a job, it is rarely possible to remember accurately what particular sections of the work looked like on previous visits. It is even more difficult when the building is complete, and is impossible once the client's stamp is put on it by occupation and use.

For maintenance purposes on completion, therefore, the client would have to rely principally on the drawings which are deposited with him and which show the general construction and service runs, etc. It is, however, inevitable that during the course of the work minor modifications, which are done for any number of reasons, will be made on site which do not affect the building and are not necessarily incorporated on these drawings. Complete photographic records of the works by a well-briefed photographer are therefore advisable throughout the job. These, while dealing with site progress on the general carcass work for the architect and quantity surveyor's records, should also be specifically related to such services or other details which will be hidden by later work. They should be taken at regular intervals to form a comprehensive record of this hidden work, the type of construction and service runs related to it with all access positions, bends, etc. They should be dated and carefully referenced to the appropriate section of building. The architect and quantity surveyor should have copies throughout the course of the work and, at the end of the contract, a complete set should be forwarded to the client for his records and maintenance purposes.

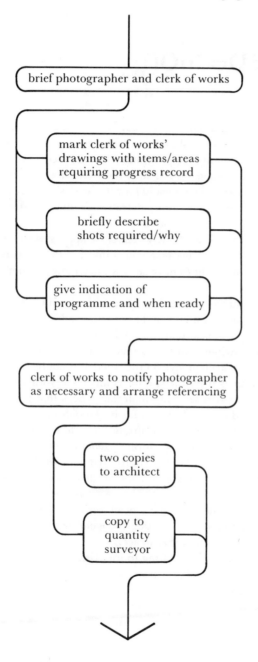

63

Site inspection

On a routine visit to the site make certain that you know what stage the job should have reached, check against the programme in advance and relate your inspection to the appropriate stage and against the clerk of works' reports. Know the order in which trades are following and how the work should be progressing. Visit frequently enough to ensure that any defective or unacceptable work is still 'accessible' for rejection. Decide in advance why you are making the visit and list what your are going to look at and why. The same applies when visiting workshops. It is too easy to go to a site because you think it is time you made a visit and miss all the things you ought to have seen while enquiring about the site agent's cold.

Deal with items you have listed first. Deal with any queries raised on site next. If you are asked anything which you do not know, admit it, find out and answer it from the office. Spot check items minutely in terms of material, workmanship and adherence to drawings; but take a tape and check the position of individual items remembering to keep an eye on the wood and not be too preoccupied with the trees. Take samples from the site for comparison with samples in the office which were obtained when selecting materials; check that tests on materials are being made in accordance with directions in the bills of quantities and that you have been notified of all results; go through the clerk of works' current report and check plant on site, materials, storage, general state of the site and existing properties. Recognize when you are confronted with work which does not meet the contract requirements that you are not entitled to accept it, and that the next visit is too late.

Do not hang about when you have dealt with all you wished to do. Do not instruct a workman direct. Instruct the site agent or clerk of works, as they are the only people there with authority to act upon such instruction under the terms of the contract; though where relating to unsatisfactory work or site error avoid doing so where onlookers might see it as casting doubt on the decisions or authority of the site agent. This applies equally to a principal architect in respect of the inspecting architect. Confirm to the contractor all points arising from the visit to the site. Send a copy to the quantity surveyor.

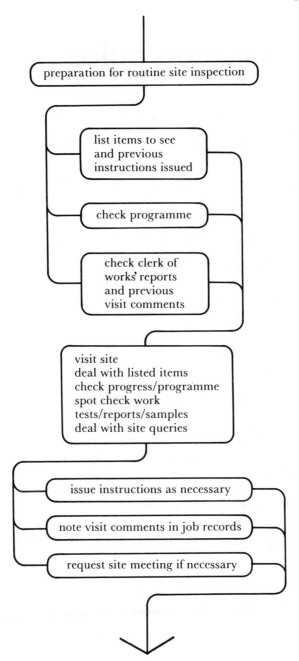

preparation for routine site inspection

list items to see
and previous
instructions issued

check programme

check clerk of
works' reports
and previous
visit comments

visit site
deal with listed items
check progress/programme
spot check work
tests/reports/samples
deal with site queries

issue instructions as necessary

note visit comments in job records

request site meeting if necessary

64

Site inspection guide

Demolition

property
    salvage.
    clearance underground.
    sealing services.
trees
    part lopping.
    underground roots.
general
    identification.
    access.
    removal.
    protection.
    programme.

Take over site

setting out
    agree levels and setting out for building(s).
    agree confines of site working area.
    spoil deposit.
notices
    check submission to local authority.
huts, plant and materials
    position (relative to later buildings where unknown to contractor).
    water.
    roads and circulation.
    protection/security.
documents
    drawings.
    programme.
    bills of quantities.
    copies of contract terms.
    weekly return forms.
    names and addresses: local authorities
                                 quantity surveyor and consultants
                                 sub-contractors

Excavation

conformity with
    drawings.
    bills of quantities.
    programme.
site work
    timbering/safety and stability.
    adjoining property.
    water clearance/sumps at base of heavy reinforcement.
    mechanical/manual removal.
    flat bed/stone removal and adequate joint pockets or bedding for drains.
    consistent bearing in foundation bases/prod or test load/check consistency
    of stratification against trial hole records.
    back-filling and ramming.
    spoil deposit.
    hard core/material size.
    thickness.

Foundations/slab

conformity with
    drawings.
    bills of quantities.
    specification and tests for piling.
    engineer's reports.
    programme.
site work
    timbering or stability.
    tanking/sumps.
    blinding/full cover to base of reinforcement.
    materials and mix.
    additives.
    reinforcement/rigidity.
    joints/stepping.
    damp proof membrane and continuity.
    defective work or material.
    samples/tests/engineer's reports.

Drainage
conformity with
>   drawings.
>   bills of quantities.
>   programme.
>   statutory requirements.

site work
>   materials/off loading/storage.
>   sizes/bed surround and mix/gradient and levels.
>   jointing/mains connections/inspection chambers/render and mix/.
>   back-fill clear of stones/full concrete cover where tree roots.
>   ancillary equipment/gullies/traps/covers/gratings.
>   defective material and workmanship/fractures in pipes, spigots or sockets/
>   protective coating intact.
>   samples and tests/services reports.

Superstructure carcass
conformity in all cases with
>   drawings.
>   bills of quantities.
>   consultant or specialist details and specification.
>   tolerances/relationships with future operations.
>   manufacturers' recommendations.
>   statutory or other consent requirements.

concrete
>   materials/mix/storage/use of cement in delivered order.
>   reinforcement—rigidity, no grease, bitumen, rust films or scales.
>   formwork/alignment/even cover/strutting and stability/tight joints.
>   method of placing/construction joints/lifts/ducts/sleeves/vibration—should
>   be no water on surface/lift cleaning—chiselled, loose cleaned off, water
>   saturated/good mortar bed before placing next lift.
>   additives/damp-proofing and continuity/protection.
>   finishes/dusting/key for plaster/throatings or weatherings.
>   defective material or workmanship/surface after stripping shuttering/
>   honey-combing/no steel or tie wire showing.
>   engineer's reports.

Superstructure carcass *(continued)*

steelwork

material/scaling/preservative.

omissions/incorrect positioning.

bolt holes which should be filled.

alignment of all members/buckling/bracing deformity.

engineer's reports.

brickwork or block partitions

off loading and stacking.

bond/alignment/rise/setting out.

internal partitions.

damp-proof courses/and continuity.

cavity ties down outwards, clear of mortar/clearance/closure/chases/ducts/sleeves.

mortar/materials/mix/pointing.

insulation and continuity.

defective material or workmanship/samples.

masonry

off loading and storage.

mortar/materials/mix/pointing.

damp proofing and continuity.

fixings/bondings/protection/defective material or workmanship.

roofing

materials/storage/off loading.

insulation continuity/batten pitch and fixing/elimination of board edge unevenness where sheet roofing over flashings/pointing or bedding/lapping or jointing/upstands/seams, etc./chases for and tucking/topping—surfaces to be dry before felt or asphalt work carried out.

pitch/fixings/firring/falls.

gutters jointing and falls/overflow levels or weirs.

throatings/weatherings/drips.

fire stops.

defective material or workmanship.

samples.

timber (plus workshop inspection)

materials/storage/protection.

evidence of preservative on prepared and site-cut materials/fireproofing/moisture content

jointing/connections/general fixing/alignment/bearings/rigidity

battens/backboards/plates/fixing pellets/grounds/ventilation arrangements/fire stops

defective material or workmanship.

samples and tests.

Superstructure carcass *(continued)*
    metalwork (plus workshop inspection)
        materials/storage.
        preservative or other treatment.
        general fixing/lugs/bolts/cramps/dowels/bedding and pointing.
        isolation from corrosive materials.
        defective material or workmanship.
    plastering/rendering and screeds
        materials/mix/storage/protection.
        preparation/key/lathings.
        battening/board fixings/scrim application/waterproofing
        surfaces and final finish/angles/making good
        screed falls/service run protection.
        defective material or workmanship.
    plumbing—external and internal
        materials and fittings/storage/protection.
        weights/gauge/sizes.
        fixings/jointing or connections/underlays/laggings or insulation/
        accessibility.
        ancillary equipment/valves/meters/overflows accessibility.
        defective material or workmanship.
        samples, tests, authority approval of installations and fittings.
    service installations (inspect with consultant where employed)
        electrical.
            materials/connections/attendance/fixings components/alignment/
            protection.
        gas heating.
            ducts/falls/covers/accessibility.
        hot water.
            equipment/action/condition of finish/relationship with other works/
            identification.
        telephone.
        mechanical services.
            tests/sample materials.
            defective material or workmanship.

Finishes

generally check

    floorings/sub-floor condition/fixing or bedding adhesion/protection/ junction strips/expansion joints/finishes.

    fittings (plus workshop inspection)/alignment/scribing/fixing/finish/ lippings.

    glazing/type/weight/thickness/quality/samples/mirror fixings/fixing or bedding.

    painting/surface condition/preparation/coats/colour/finish/samples.

    polishing/surface condition/preparation/finish/samples.

    ironmongery/fixings/action/housings/finish/alignment/master systems.

External works

conformity with

    drawings/bills of quantities/programme.

site works

    roads/pavings/materials/base/consolidation/construction joints/falls/ finish.

    lighting/cable trench excavation/base mix.

    ground preparation and levels/seeding/planting/turfing/protection.

    walls/fences/damp proof courses/copings/foundation or base/mix and materials.

65

Certificate procedure

The quantity surveyor prepares valuations at the periods and in accordance with the terms and conditions laid down in the contract, and submits these to the architect for his guidance in issuing certificates for payments on account to the contractor. Where no quantity surveyor is employed, the valuations are prepared by the architect. The valuation comprises the works on site, materials delivered to the site but not fixed; nominated sub-contractors' and nominated suppliers' work, daywork sheets where applicable, and any other substantiating evidence. It will also itemize the principal sums due to the contractor, and noting which sums are included to be passed to sub-contractors for works to date, and will note the retention held until completion.

It is exceedingly important that the valuation is a factual and accurate document, as it may, in the case where a contractor or sub-contractor enters into a state of liquidation, be the basis of decision on how much a client can claim to have bought if the receivers take possession of material and plant on site which is not fixed.

Where a sub-contractor has completed work in the early stages of a very long contract, it would be unjust to hold a retention figure on his work until the end. Arrangements should be made with the quantity surveyor to release the full amount of this retention at the point in the contract where the sub-contractor's liabilities would normally end, though in doing so due account must be taken of indemnity of the general contractor by the sub-contractor.

Copies of the valuation are sent to the architect and the contractor by the quantity surveyor. It is necessary to obtain clearance from consultants that the work under their direction is satisfactory. The certificate for payment, made on the standard form related to the agreement in use, is released by the architect to the contractor within the time stated in the Articles of Agreement. At the same time, the sub-contractors whose work has been included should be notified of the amount released against their accounts and asked to submit receipts when the sum is received from the contractor.

The client and quantity surveyor are automatically informed by copy, when the certificate is released. On release of the first certificate, it is as well to describe the procedure to the client for his information, and to advise him of the period in which he should honour the certificate in accordance with the Articles of Agreement.

The contractor submits the certificate to the client for payment direct. It should not be paid through the architect's office.

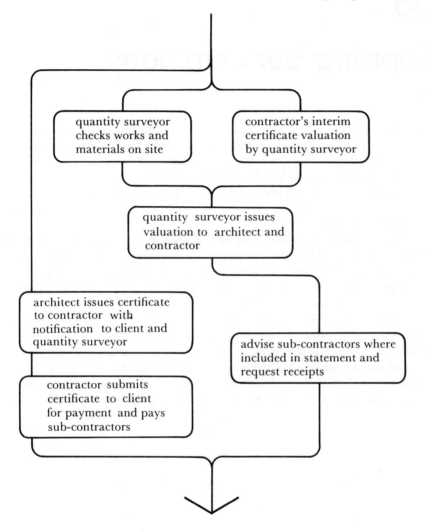

66

Topping out ceremony

The origins of this ceremony seem to be lost in history, but it is performed all over the world in one form or another and is traditionally associated with the point at which the topmost stone is to be fixed to the building. In its simplest form this act is signalled by a branch of evergreen being hoisted to the top of the building, and a toast drunk by everyone on the site to celebrate the completion of the structure of the building.

There have been many variations of this over the years depending upon the period in history or its location. On an open site the evergreen is frequently thrown to the ground to be burnt, as the last part of a ceremony to ward off any evil influences, and it is claimed that when sacrifices were associated with the event, it has involved building the architect into the structure . . .

In practical terms it establishes the point at which the client is able to thank and pay his own respects to the men who have actually been constructing the building, and it is, and should be, his party for all the workmen on the site. The space allocated to that part of the event should therefore be fairly generous. The ceremony itself takes place at the highest point, so may have to be confined to a fairly small platform that will hold the immediate participants, principal guests and photographers. On the other hand, where it is a flat roof area, the entire site personnel can be accommodated for the party and the ceremony.

The client as host will be responsible for the list of guests over and above the general invitation to all site staff, and will welcome all visitors on arrival. Plenty of time should be allowed between the arrival time and the ceremony to permit people to get from the street—possibly by hoist—to the top of a building which is still essentially a shell, and special safety arrangements may have to be made to conduct this operation.

On this occasion the architect explains the background and introduces the ceremony to the assembly. The client then thanks and congratulates all the people concerned with the construction, and the builder generally responds and invites the principal guest to undertake the topping out. This is done by placing in position the last brick, tile or shovel of concrete as appropriate; the site agent will have made arrangements for this to be done in whatever way is simplest and least likely to fail. When this is done the evergreen is hoisted, and beer, the traditional drink for a topping out, is distributed for the proposal of the toast and the equally traditional three cheers.

67

Practical completion inspection

There are two stages to the completion of a building contract. The first stage, described as practical completion, is the acceptance by the architect of the building as complete and ready for occupation. The second stage is completion proper, which usually comes six months afterwards, when the building is inspected for defects, the necessary corrective work carried out and the final account settled.

Inspections for practical completion and defects liability should be careful and detailed. It is advisable to follow a fixed pattern in inspecting the building and, if necessary, to do it in several short periods rather than one long one, when through weariness or irritability the inspection may be prejudiced.

Bear in mind, when making your inspection for practical completion, that this is not the opportunity for catching up on points you should have noticed during normal site inspections, but that it should be specifically concerned with the correct operation of all equipment, completion of all finishes, and defective or omitted items. To obtain a consistent result the inspection should be made with an inspection schedule containing broad headings of floors, walls, ceiling, doors, windows, electrical equipment, services equipment, sanitary ware, joinery, or other items, depending upon the character of the building. The later, defects liability, inspection can be a second stage of the same schedule. Detailed consideration will need to be given to such things as:

General cleanliness of all surfaces.
Adhesion of plaster, tiles or other applied surfaces.
Completed decorative finish according to schedule.
Screws and fixings secure.
Signwriting or notices completed.
Mechanical and other services tested.
Ironmongery operation, and keys handed over.
Correct light fittings and lamps.
Electric switch plates on and secure.
Fire-fighting equipment complete.
Sanitary fittings complete, clean and working.
Gully gratings, etc., in position.
Doors, windows operating full arc.
Joinery junctions, scribings, etc., finished.
Earlier defects and making good generally finished.

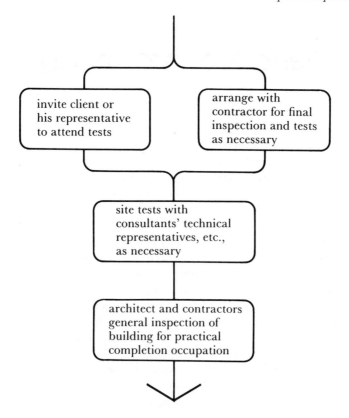

The contractor should arrange for the final tests to be carried out on mechanical and other services either before or during this inspection. Ensure that you or the appropriate consultant attends all tests. Your client should be invited to attend or send a representative so that he will be fully acquainted with the operation of the services and equipment. Consultants must confirm acceptance of all work under their direction. Finally, check escape routes and any other conditions of consents, including party structure or adjoining owners' work.

68

Maintenance information

Before the building is occupied, sub-contractors, suppliers and manufacturers should be asked to provide instructions for the best care of their materials and equipment so that the information can be passed to the client. These should cover items such as flooring materials, finishes to all internal surfaces, or anything requiring regular maintenance.

Although the architect will request through the general contractor that sub-contractors deal with the correction of any failure in material during the liability period, the client, after the contract has been settled and the obligation discharged, will need to be able to contact these firms direct for advice on anything arising related to the work. It is important, then, that with the instructions, your client is given the firm's name, address, telephone number and, if possible, the name of the person who dealt with the contract, or who knows the history of the work on site and how it was carried out. For instance, your client does not want to have to contact you for a new set of keys.

To this information add the full set of progress photographs taken throughout the course of the work showing the construction of the building in stages.

As well as ensuring that all the equipment and services in the building have been tested under the direction of the services consultant, as well as colour coded and labelled, before handing over to your client, arrange for him or his maintenance staff to be shown the positions of all mains, intake points, distribution boxes, isolation valves, etc., and how to operate mechanical services, emergency or fire-fighting equipment.

This is the point at which the health and safety file should be handed to the client for his own and future user's records.

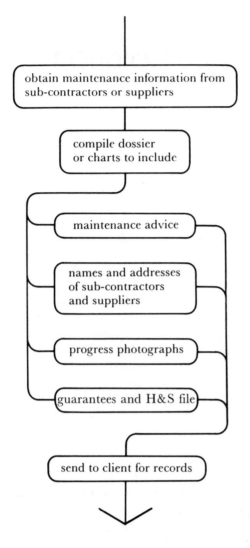

obtain maintenance information from
sub-contractors or suppliers

compile dossier
or charts to include

maintenance advice

names and addresses
of sub-contractors
and suppliers

progress photographs

guarantees and H&S file

send to client for records

69

Practical completion

Practical completion is the stage at which a building can be said to be in a state ready for occupation by the client without inconvenience. This is probably the most difficult clause in the contract to interpret fairly to both client and contractor. It is excessively inconvenient and frustrating for a client who has moved into a new building to find sections of an otherwise complete building in need of making good, or with a couple of light fittings missing. On the other hand, it is impossible to say the building is not capable of being occupied. It is often equally inconvenient for the contractor to try to complete the work while the building is occupied and people are wanting him out of the way, with the result that it is almost impossible to get a contractor back once the client is installed.

It is essential, therefore, that the architect insists on completion offering beneficial occupation before the builder leaves the site. This means that the building is practically complete pending settlement of the defects at the end of the defects liability period stated in the Articles of Agreement. Certification of practical completion is certification of completion as far as liquidated and ascertained damages are concerned, and this certificate has the effect, where appropriate to the particular articles being used, of releasing in a complementary certificate of payment to the contractor the agreed proportion of the retention figure as stated in the Articles of Agreement.

When the contractor has overrun the agreed contract time, including any extension of time that has been granted, he should be informed that the work should reasonably have been completed and therefore, as from that particular date, the liquidated damages clause will come into operation and that future certificates will be endorsed 'subject to whatever may be the rights of the employer under *the liquidated damages* clause of the contract', or other similar qualification.

The architect must in no way prejudice the rights of his client to invoke this clause, and for this reason he should endorse the certificates.

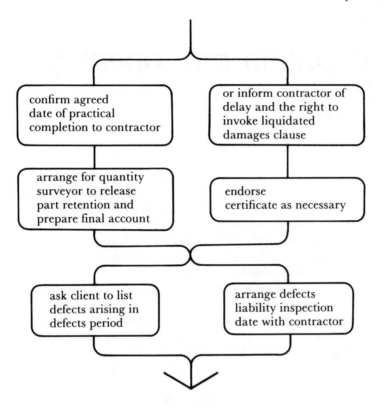

70

Occupation and opening ceremony

As a rule the client who has lived with the construction site since its origins recognizes and feels part of the achievement and in retrospect, has probably quite enjoyed the process. Regrettably however there is a tendency for occupants who have not grown up with it to be somewhat petulant about teething troubles, particularly if they have lived through the defects period with the need for doors to be eased and air-conditioning to be balanced.

The architect's hunted behaviour in dealing with this is probably part of the vacuum he inevitably feels on completing a job which has occupied him fully for a number of years. It probably also accounts for his sense of personal injury when typists stick calendars on the newly decorated walls with adhesive tape, after he has spent three months avoiding arbitration with the general contractor in establishing the client's right to have the walls totally redecorated after the defects period.

If a client decides to have an opening ceremony it will generally be some time after occupation of the building, when it is looking clean, trim and in good working order. With a large company, the event frequently contains a strong element of public relations, and the architect's involvement will be minimal in terms of arrangements. It may require the preparation of a brief description of the building, its services, its principal components and its vital statistics, which may or may not include the construction time and cost. A credits list will generally be asked for but there may be reluctance to publish any more than names of the principal consultants.

This is a full-scale client's event, and an architect must recognize that the process by which the building emerged is the last thing which will be in the client's mind, or be of significance to the ceremony. The process is generally acknowledged in the ceremony, but only in passing, and the architect or anyone from the design and construction team is unlikely to be invited to participate except as an observer. The architect's job has been completed long before this event takes place; so in client terms there is, strictly speaking, no need for him to be involved at all.

In the end the architect has both to acknowledge that the building belongs to someone else, and to learn not to object to its being occupied by the people who paid for it. The opening ceremony quite clearly declares and confirms the occupant as the owner of the building.

71
Defects liability

On practical completion of the contract, the date for the defects liability inspection as predetermined by the defects period entered in the contract should be decided and the contractor informed. Inform your client of this date and ask him to note defects which arise before that date and which may not be apparent during the actual defects inspection. Your client should also be informed (and it should be borne in mind during your own inspection) that defects do not include damage caused by him or his staff during the move into the building or since occupation, and it is advisable to quote the clause in the contract which deals with this particular item, in order that he does not expect the contractor to make the building brand new again. Before the period elapses, ask for his list of items discovered to be defective during occupation or use of the building and incorporate it in your schedule for inspection.

The inspection of the property should then be related to the inspection schedule as used for the practical completion inspection, in order that the inspection can be made methodically and so that you can be sure that everything has been included. Copies of the completed schedule of defects should be prepared for the contractor, the quantity surveyor and the client. After consultation with your client, arrange with the contractor the dates on which he will start and finish the work and instruct him accordingly. On completion of the work, a second and final inspection should be made which goes through the schedule item by item. This inspection together with the final clearance from consultants is vital as a final certificate cannot be issued unless all defects are remedied. The quantity surveyor should be instructed that, when the contractor's liabilities have been certified as complete, the final statement of account should be issued and to release the remainder of the retention.

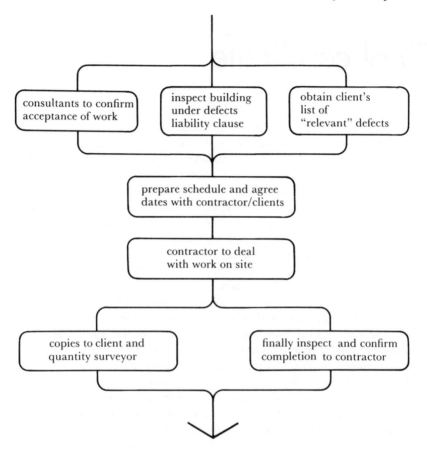

72
Final certificate

The quantity surveyor's statement of final account for the work will be an itemized statement in the form arranged at the beginning of the contract. It should take into account the variations to the work as ordered from time to time throughout the contract in order that the client can relate all his previous record copies to the relevant section of the account. It should set the original provisional sums or prime cost assessments, made when compiling the bills of quantities, against the actual sums which have been expended on the appropriate item. It will take into account extensions of time, claims, contingencies, etc.

It will be presented through the architect to the client as a statement agreed with the contractor on the client's behalf by his quantity surveyor as his agent, and will represent the true financial statement of account for the total works. The architect's duty, on condition that he has satisfied himself that it is a fair interpretation of respective liabilities under the terms laid down in the Articles of Agreement (which is the extent of his authority in the agreement of the final account), is to recommend the client to pay this in settlement of the contract.

The architect, therefore, if satisfied with the work, issues his final certificate (marked *Final*) to the contractor when passing the final account to his client. It is not a document on which discussion takes place with a view to negotiating outstanding difficulties. If defects of any kind exist when the final certificate is due the certificate must not be issued. The issue of a 'final' certificate assumes that everything is acceptable. Signed copies of the account should be sent to both the client and contractor.

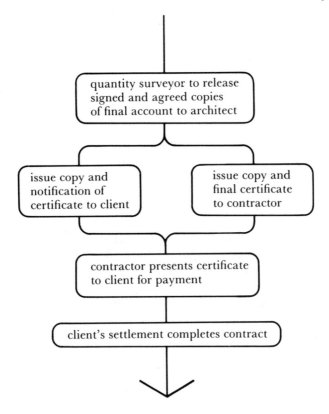

73
Final fees

Depending upon the original terms of appointment for consultants you may have, from time to time, received interim statements for fees from the quantity surveyor and consultants to be forwarded to the client. These you will have verified as being in accordance with the original agreed terms and passed on to your client for payment direct. Ensure now that all consultants have submitted their final fees and that these have all been settled before submitting your own final account for fees to the client. Your own final account should describe the stages through which the contract has passed since submitting your interim accounts and should include all outstanding expenses. It should be noted as the 'final statement of account' for fees.

Forward the original contract documents to your client for his records together with a set of drawings of the building brought up to date 'as-built', the maintenance information and associated photographs and inform him that you intend to keep all other documents relevant to the contract for six years from the date of practical completion where a contract is signed, and twelve years where executed under seal. After this they will be destroyed. Tell the contractor of these arrangements. You may find the client has become so used to telephoning you about sundry items since moving into the building that it is necessary to write diplomatically but firmly informing him that this represents the termination of your present services to the contract.

Request permission to use photographs or drawings of the work if required for publication, exhibition, or when asked by new clients for illustrations of previous work.

If your client asks, it is as well to know that you hold automatic copyright to the building's 'artistic merit' and any drawings etc., prepared in developing the scheme, until fifty years after your death. The client, in purchasing the service, has a right to use the drawings, which have been prepared to convey information on its construction, for that purpose.

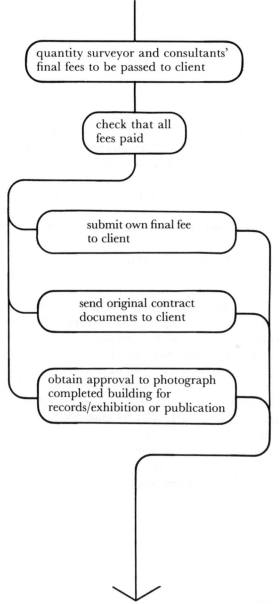

74

Records

On the conclusion of the contract, set aside for record purposes a comprehensive set of photographs of the completed building as well as those taken during the works. Photographs of the completed building should be taken by a competent architectural photographer after a careful site briefing. Your client's permission should be obtained before taking these photographs. Photographs are important for office records as potential clients will often ask to see illustrations of previous work. Only release drawings of previous contracts when you have the client's prior permission to do so.

Should photographs be required subsequently for press publication, a good set taken at this time will ensure that your client is not inconvenienced by further photographic visits.

Kept with the photographs should be a final analysis of the job in terms of total cost, cost by superficial area, length of contract, number of assistants and cost to the office, and a short report on the work including the approach to the problem and your recommendations. Notes should also be incorporated giving information on the consultants, contractor, sub-contractors and suppliers. To abstract any of this information, even six months after completion of the contract, means endless research unless these records are compiled and, if the information is required ten years after, would otherwise be impossible.

You may be asked by the contractor, or a sub-contractor, for the use of your name in advertising material. You should first ask your client whether he has any objection, and agree only on condition that your name is used as architect to the particular building, and that you may agree the copy or the proofs before they are actually passed for publication.

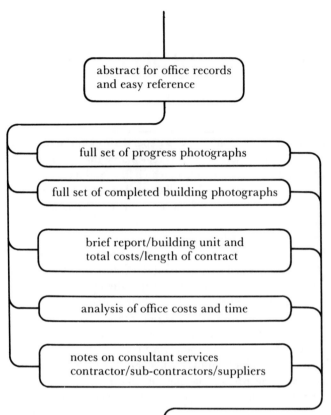

abstract for office records
and easy reference

full set of progress photographs

full set of completed building photographs

brief report/building unit and
total costs/length of contract

analysis of office costs and time

notes on consultant services
contractor/sub-contractors/suppliers

75
Recommendations

Just as at the outset of the contract you depended upon the opinion of referees before taking preliminary decisions, it is reasonable that at the end of a contract you should offer to be a referee to a firm which has produced a good result, given a good service to the client, or whose liaison throughout the work with all the people involved has assured good progress and sound relations.

Many smaller commercial firms depend a great deal upon recommendations from past clients for further business. It is as much your duty to acknowledge a good service at the end of a contract as it was to recommend the firm to the client in the first place. When writing to offer your services as a referee for future enquiries, it is also reasonable to remember that the firm deserves to know which of their employees produced the result on their behalf, together with any comments you may have on the service, and information which would be of importance to the man running the business, or the way in which he conducts a future operation. Similarly, you should inform a firm if you consider their service to have been bad. As it is highly unlikely that the client, architect, contractor and sub-contractors will meet again on one job, the benefit to others of this local criticism is about the only form of post-mortem open to the building industry.

It is easy to forget, during the client's move into the premises, that the individuals, who have been working on the building since it was a heap of mud, are being evicted at the very point where they are beginning to be proud of their finishes, and before they even get the opportunity to stand back and admire their work. Acknowledgement of good results by individuals should not be overlooked.

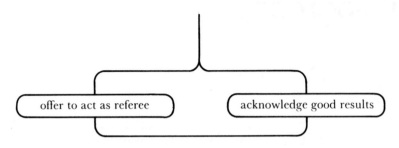

Bibliography

Addleson, Lyall, *Building Failures*, Butterworth Architecture, 3rd edn, 1992

Addleson, Lyall and Rice, Colin, *Performance of Materials in Buildings*, Butterworth-Heinemann, paperback edition, 1994

Association of Consultant Architects, *ACA Contract Documents* (various items), Architectural Press

Blanc, Alan, *Internal Components*, Longman (Mitchell's building series), 1994

Bowyer, Jack, *Guide to Domestic building Surveys*, Architectural Press, 3rd edn, 1978

Burberry, Peter, *Environment and Services*, Longman (Mitchell's building series), 7th edn, 1992

Cecil, Ray, *Professional Liability*, Legal Studies Publishing, 3rd edn, 1991

Chappell, David and Powell-Smith, Vincent, *JCT Intermediate Form of Contract: a Practical Guide*, 2nd edn, 1991

Cox, Stanley H., *The Architect's Guide to the JCT Intermediate Form (IFC 84)*, RIBA Publications, 2nd edn, 1989

Cresswell, H. B., *The Honeywood File and Honeywood Settlement*, Architectural Press, 1986

Davis, Lawrence, *Guide to the Building Regulations*, 1991, Butterworth Architecture, 1992

Davis, Langdon and Everest (editors), *Spon's A + B: Architects' Builders' Price Book, 1994*, Spon, 119th edn, 1993

Dean, Yvonne, *Finishes*, Longman (Mitchell's building series), 3rd edn, 1989

Department of the Environment/Welsh Office, *The Building Regulations 1991*, HMSO 1992 (for complete pack including manual and approved documents)

Doran, D. K., *Construction Materials Reference Book*, Butterworth-Heinemann, paperback edition, 1994

Elder, A. J., *The Rubicon File*, Architectural Press, 1980

Everett, Alan, *Materials*, Longman (Mitchell's building series) 5th edn, 1994

Foster, Jack, *Structure and Fabric*, Longman (Mitchell's building series), Part 1 and 2, 5th edn, 1994

Greenstreet, Bob and Chappell, David, *Legal and Contractural Procedures for Architects*, Butterworth Architecture, 4th edn, 1994

Jones, Vincent, *Neufert Architects' Data*, BSP Professional Books, 2nd edn, 1980

Keating, Donald, *Law and Practice of Building Contracts*, Sweet and Maxwell, 1982

Martin, P. L. and Oughton, D. R., *Faber and Kell's Heating and Air Conditioning of Buildings*, Butterworth-Heinemann, 8th edn, 1994

McEvoy, Michael, *External Components*, Longman (Mitchell's building series), 1994

Melville, I. A. and Gordon, I. A., *The Repair and Maintenance of Homes*, Estates Gazette, 1973

Osbourn, D., *Introduction to Building*, Longman (Mitchell's building series), 1989

Parris, J., *The Standard Form of Building Contract: JCT 1980*, Granada, 1982

RIBA, *Handbook of Architectural Practice and Management*, RIBA Publications, 4th edn, 1980

Royal Institution of Chartered Surveyors, *Party Wall Legislation and Procedure*, Surveyor's Publications

Speaight, Anthony and Stone, Gregory (editors), *Architect's Legal Handbook*, Butterworth Architecture, 5th edn, 1990

Staveley, H. S., and Glover, P. V., *Building Surveys*, Buterworth-Heinemann, 2nd edn, 1990

Styles, Keith, *Working Drawings Handbook*, Butterworth Architecture, 2nd edn, 1986

Tutt, Patricia and Adler, David (editors), *New Metric Handbook*, Butterworth Architecture, revised 1981

Williams, Alan (editor), *Specification 1994* (current edition of a standard work), Emap Business Publishing, 1994